ATTITUDE
RESEARCH
UNDER THE SUN

ATTITUDE RESEARCH UNDER THE SUN

JOHN EIGHMEY, editor
Northwestern University

Proceedings Series

222 S. Riverside Plaza-Chicago, Illinois 60606-(312) 648-0536

Library of Congress Cataloging in Publication Data

Attitude Research Conference, 9th, Tarpon Springs,
   Fla., 1978.
   Attitude research under the sun.

   Bibliography: p.
   1. Attitude (Psychology)—Testing—Congresses.
2. Marketing research—Congresses.   3. Consumers—
Attitudes—Congresses.   I. Eighmey, John, 1944–
II. Title.
HF5415.2.A773   1978   658.8'34   78-13992
ISBN 0-87757-115-5

TABLE OF CONTENTS

FOREWORD

Attitude Research Under the Sun is the proceedings of the AMA's 1978 Attitude Research Conference. The conference was held in Tarpon Springs, Florida, in the conference facilities of the Innisbrook Resort and Country Club.

The organization of these proceedings follows the conference program as set forth by Joe Plummer, the 1978 conference chairman. The proceedings begin with the paper given by Burleigh Gardner, the featured speaker for the conference.

My thanks go to Rita Lambros for preparing the camera-ready copy.

John Eighmey
Medill School of Journalism
Northwestern University

INTRODUCTION

Although the 1978 Attitude Research Conference had no official "theme," the objective of the conference was to explore in an interdisciplinary fashion some newer areas such as attitude trend research, some neglected areas such as content analysis, and some areas of broad interest such as attitude models. An effort was made to present a program of fresh faces and to represent a diversity of scholarly and business viewpoints.

The papers contained in these proceedings reflect the interdisciplinary nature of the conference and demonstrate the high levels of professionalism, creativity, and hard work given by each speaker. Their efforts deserve consideration by anyone concerned with attitude research and its potential to better human understanding by marketers, educators, advertisers, and policy-makers.

A number of speakers (Gardner, Skelly, Davis and Roscho) raised some vital concerns about the assumptions, methodology and interpretation of public opinion surveys and attitude research. They indicated that such surveys will be a major factor in the near future of attitude research and that it is a very under-researched area in terms of sampling, question development, reliability and models of analysis. Much research today, in the views of these researchers, seems to be poorly designed, not integrated empirically or theoretically, and widely misused by the popular press and decision-makers.

Several of the speakers suggested some very fresh and useful approaches to some tried and true areas of attitude research such as attitude models (Myers and Woelfel), retailing (Tigert) and content analysis (Van Tubergen, Guttman and Reynolds). I urge the reader to consider these creative approaches to attitude research and problem-solving.

And, finally, the speakers in the sessions dealing with attitude research and advertising (Lastovicha, Schlinger, Fiedler and Hixon) challenged the widely held notions of attitude change as a meaningful model for most advertising research. Lastovicha approached the issue from the standpoint of low involvement theory and a variety of learning models. Schlinger presented the results of years of copy research on attitudinal response measures and found a multi-dimensional response structure quite useful to advertising professionals. And Fiedler and Hixon demonstrated dramatically and creatively that advertising for the print media must be approached differently than advertising for television.

It was our hope to have a stimulating and enjoyable conference. I believe we did. It is also our hope that these
proceedings will be stimulating and useful to its readers in
advancing the state of the art in attitude research.

In closing I would like to give special thanks to everyone
who helped bring the conference and these proceedings to life
-- John Snow, Lynn Shaper, Ray Suh, Cal Gage, Ed Freeman, Bill
Wells, Stu Agres, Janie Zeyen, John Eighmey and all the
speakers.

Joseph T. Plummer
1978 Conference Chairman

NUMBERS ARE NOT ENOUGH

Burleigh B. Gardner, Ph.D.
Social Research, Inc.

Viewing the current practices and results in attitude research, I feel that the work has reached a plateau, with little
that is new in conceptualization or evidence of progress toward
better understanding of the phenomenon under examination. It
brings to mind an old military drill, "In place -- MARCH!"
Whether it is one man or 1,000 in the unit, they expend a lot
of energy but never go anywhere.

In thinking about the state of attitude research, I am reminded in my early training as an engineer. I remember at that
time reading an article about the turn of the century by an
eminent scientist, who said that there was nothing new in
physics, no great new challenges, just a lot of work to be done
applying the known principles of Newtonian physics. I also remember a professor of physics who said that only a handful of
physicists could understand the Theory of Relativity and Einstein's equations. Yet today, any young physicist must understand and be able to apply the Theory of Relativity, and without this conceptual system we probably would not have nuclear
energy or computers, or be able to explore either outer space
or the basic structure of matter.

However, Newtonian physics was a conceptual system perfectly adequate for building bridges or navigating the oceans
or predicting the orbits of the planets. For the practical
needs of everyday life it was quite adequate and still is. As
a conceptual system it is not wrong, just limited. It enabled
man to understand many phenomena, and the phenomena it did not
explain could, for most purposes, be ignored.

Also, there was a large body of older scientists who re-
fused to accept the new concepts. They had grown up and built
careers on Newtonian physics and were not about to accept something new. This was reminiscent of the early Ptolemaic philosophers who believed that the world was the center of the universe, and when later men such as Copernicus and Galileo sought
to prove otherwise, they were disclaimed and branded as here-
tics.

Unfortunately, in our present state of attitude research,
there is not a problem of replacing an inadequate conceptual
system with a better one. We do not have an articulated conceptual system to begin with. Today, the social scientists

are enamoured of numbers and counting. They forget that they are examining one aspect of behaviour of people and are too often satisfied if they can count responses to a given set of questions ("Who will you vote for?" "How is Carter doing his job?" "Which ad do you prefer?"), feed them to a computer, and regard the final output as a truth. Rarely do they stop and ask, "What lies behind the numbers?" (You will notice that I am using the word "attitudes" in the broadest sense, as verbal expressions which may range from deep-seated and stable beliefs -- such as the beliefs about the Untouchables in the caste system of India -- to temporary preferences, as when one chooses luncheon from a menu.)

However, we have an overwhelming amount of information and measurements, especially in the area of consumer attitude research. But where are the conceptual systems by which we can fit it all together? As long as we have the information we think we need for an immediate problem, we never seem to wonder beyond these needs. It is as though we were studying beaches only by counting grains of sand, and never wondering why they are there at all.

I want to say something about the problem of seeing beyond our established frame of reference or way of thinking, to bring in new ideas or ways of thinking. Recently, Edwin H. Land, founder of Polaroid, published an article in the latest <u>Harvard Magazine</u> in which he discussed some recent research findings on the perceptual process [1]. Although he was primarily talking about the visual process and the perception of color, he concludes that what we perceive as what we call the "external" world is a complex reaction within the brain to the stimuli brought to it. He says in part:

> "It is not error in grand policies that endangers
> our planet, but the imprisonment in our own minds,
> which, if set free, would guide us individually
> first of all and collectively after all."

Another author who speaks to the point of the constraints placed upon us by our habitual ways of thinking is George J. Goodman, who writes under the pen-name of Adam Smith. In his last book, <u>Powers of Mind</u>, he discusses the limitations imposed by our "paradigms" or conceptual schemes [5]. He says:

> "A paradigm is a shared set of assumptions...the
> paradigm explains the world to us and helps us
> predict its behaviour...
>
> "Our scientific paradigm has produced the absolute
> and splendid technological achievements of Western

2

man. But it leaves us with a problem, that is we
have an unconscious tendency to consider as 'real'
that which can be easily measured and less real,
or unreal, that which can't...

"But quantification has not noticeably increased
our understanding of dreams or feelings, and some
observers think we exclude those of our perceptions that don't match the paradigm because that's
what we were trained to do."

This makes our paradigm seem to be a highly rational and recognized conceptual system. Edwin Land, in his paper on perception, contends that the way we perceive the world is a learned
system but its base is deep in the inner workings of the brain.

Land does not restrict himself to the perception of color.
He holds that the mind is besieged by a chaos of sensory input.
The mind gives structure to this chaos; it interprets certain
patterns of input as colors, as objects, as everything we think
of as the external world, yet it only exists in the form we
perceive because of our minds.

Now, when we talk about attitudes, we are talking about
more constructs of the mind. When we do attitude research we
are trying to probe these constructs of the mind as they are
expressed in response to our questions. But usually all we
really know are the questions we asked and the responses we
get. It reminds me of asking a four-year-old how the lights
work and he says, "You push the switch and they come on." Are
we to be satisfied with this level of understanding of how the
mind works and/or how attitudes are formed?

The statement that the world is more complicated than we
think it to be brings me to a criticism of much attitude research or survey research. When you send out questionnaires
asking people to choose among alternatives, you have data which
only reflects the world as you see it. Years ago, when Lloyd
Warner first reported his research showing that our society has
a social class structure, the findings were not accepted by
many. I remember hearing one well-known pollster say, "I have
conducted national polls for 20 years and have never seen any
evidence of social class." Of course he hadn't -- the data he
collected and the way he organized it did not allow such an
undemocratic reality as social class to stand up and be seen.
His view of our society was an artifact of his mind and his
methods. He could not say, "That's an interesting view of the
structure of society. How can I test it out on a national
sample?" Yet others did; the original research on one community was replicated in many others. Also there are methods for

approximating social class on large samples which can be used in any survey. Yet how often do you see national surveys reported that show the responses by social class as a useful variable?

Today, many of the social sciences -- sociology, social psychology, political science -- have become so bemused with numbers that the student is not trained to see the people behind the numbers. The research techniques are designed to produce numbers that can be turned over to others. Thus, the Ph.D. may get his degree without ever interacting with those he is studying; they are just items on a questionnaire and numbers to be manipulated by machine.

With this, I disagree heartily. To understand attitudes, you must understand people. For a social anthropologist, the best training for understanding people is to immerse yourself in their culture, live where they live, listen to them, observe and try to see the patterns of their lives and the beliefs and sentiments that give their lives meaning. You are always seeking to see behind the behaviour to the structure which it expresses.

I was taught by an unusual group at Harvard: Lloyd Warner in anthropology, Elton Mayo and Lawrence J. Henderson in the Harvard Business School. Working with them, I studied the works of some of the great thinkers, researchers and conceptualizers -- Malinowski, Radcliff-Brown, Piaget, Durkheim, Freud, Jung, Adler, and many more. As our group studied, we were constantly in the field in Yankee City, interviewing, observing, trying to find and understand the structure and dynamics of that one community. We took to heart the creed expressed by Lawrence J. Henderson of the Harvard Business School, a physiological chemist and director of its Fatigue Laboratory. He said that:

"For the understanding of such complex phenomena... both theory and practice were necessary conditions and the method of Hippocrates was the only method that had ever succeeded widely and generally:

"The physician must have first, intimate, habitual, intuitive familiarity with things; secondly, systematic knowledge of things; and thirdly, an effective way of thinking about things." [4]

I have mentioned before the passion for numbers. By quantifying a survey and reducing it to neat computer output, we give an illusion of reality, of hard data. Yet, all the time it is only a counting of responses of human minds to questions

4

designed by human minds. For some purposes, such as predicting elections, this quantification is adequate, and the experts have a good record in prediction. However, for other purposes, such as guiding a creative department in producing an advertisement, tables of numbers merely obscure the reality of the people behind the numbers. They hide the complexities of human thought that came up with the answers to the questions given.

That is why, in recent years, consumer research has gone in two directions: focus groups, in which a small group of consumers express their views, and quantitative surveys using volumes of simplistic data. Both are inadequate to give us an understanding of how the mind works and how attitudes are formed. However, the focus groups give creative people a sense of the human realities which are absent from the quantitative surveys.

I can reduce my criticisms to four general areas:

1. Attitude and consumer research is too concerned with superficialities. It only wants to count the light switches.

2. It is not concerned with how the mind functions below the superficialities.

3. Its practioners are too engrossed in the day-to-day counting to be able to spend much thought or effort in interpretation of what the numbers mean.

4. There is no agreed-on conceptual system or even limited hypothesis which can be tested again and again by observation of human behaviour. Only thus can we build a firm structure or knowledge which can lead us to better concepts and to applications.

These are extreme overstatements, but if one examines most of the research that goes out today, they are too often true except for occasional unique situations.

Now I want to say something in defense of the practitioners. First of all, the researchers, whether in-house or in research suppliers, must first serve their clients -- the marketing people or other executives. These people, often untrained in research of any kind, can use only simplistic research and feel most comfortable with tables of numbers. They are not able to, or interested in, committing budgets for difficult research with no immediate payout in practical action. Thus, the researchers are trapped in a situation which neither stimulates serious research nor provides support for it. As David Ogilvy recently said: "It is rare for anybody except the top man to think further ahead than next year." [2]

What about those of you in academia? You are expected to do research and publish, some small studies or use your students and pick away with small or short-term studies. When we consider the level of effort, both brains and facilities, and time that Edwin Land had to apply to understand how we perceive color, we cannot expect rapid development from our academic brothers.

Another handicap is that the vast bulk of the research done is proprietary. One company has been studying employee attitudes for 30 years, but the researchers have been permitted to publish only one paper. It is as if the development of drugs were left to individual doctors who had to make their living at the same time (of course, there is some of this, and these doctors are usually quacks). Instead, in medicine there is a growing pool of knowledge with individuals as well as groups contributing.

I must say that I get the impression that there is no history. I am told the students feel that anything published a decade ago is old-fashioned and useless. As a result, they are continually reinventing the wheel.

Probably the most advanced field of attitude research is in the study of employee attitudes. I have been active in this work for over 40 years, doing both intensive research and development and applied research on specific organization problems. We can now take a questionnaire survey of an organization, measure the level of morale and identify problem spots and the source of the problems. In this work the clients want not only diagnosis but also workable prescriptions as to what to do about problems. We find that the employee complaint is often a reaction to a subjective discontent and we must be careful not to confuse the expression of discontent with the underlying causes.

In this field we have developed concepts which can both help explain data and also predict results of actions. We can then tell management what to do to adjust the system and the reactions of people. In this work we are dealing with a limited social system whose structure can be readily examined, and we can determine a course of action. It usually requires changing the behaviour of people in specific positions in the social system.

However, even this field of attitude research has a long way to go before it has an adequate conceptual base as well as an understanding of practical applications which can serve the needs of society.

However, critical as I sound, I feel that there are enough concerned practitioners that we can expect to get off our present plateau and start climbing again.

I want to speak now of the positive side and developments which can point to a greater future. One is the work in what we call "Life Style Research." Although this has been going on for years under many labels, it seems to me to be making the greatest advances using methods which I have seen used by Leo Burnett and which was recently the basis for a talk by Joe Plummer to the A.N.A. [3]. As many of you know, Bill Wells, now Vice President of Research at Needham, Harper & Steers, was an early proponent of, and was active in, developing Life Style studies when he was at the University of Chicago.

I won't try to trace the heritage of this work, but its roots are many. The original work on social class was a major step away from the classifications of people by simple demographics to types more relevant to their personal values and motives and more useful for predicting behaviour. In recent years we have seen many other attempts at classifying people through techniques under labels such as "psychographics," but I believe the current Life Style approach is the most comprehensive and is proving its value in helping creative people understand their audiences.

The idea of classifying people by some attitudinal or behaviour types is nothing new. In research it has been widely practiced on a problem-by-problem basis. For example, I recently saw a study by Yankelovich for General Mills in which he classifies parents are permissive or authoritarian and shows how the two types differ in child-rearing attitudes. However, the possibility of developing broader classifications into which these more specialized types can be fitted would be a major advance.

However, we can go on endlessly in segmenting the market or developing life style typologies. Ultimately, every person is an individual who differs in some degree from all others, and to carry segmentation to that extreme would be useless. However, some users are finding the present Life Style Analysis of value in the everyday business of advertising. In Chicago, both Needham, Harper & Steers and Leo Burnett are using it to help their creative people understand their audiences and assist in media decisions. But they do not find this a magic approach which supplants the more usual forms of research.

Although the present work shows great promise, it is at a

7

very pragmatic level. We administer an elaborate questionnaire and use some form of factor or cluster analysis to establish groups of responses to which we give a label. But where is the conceptual system which encompasses and tries to explain the meanings of these groups and the social and psychological system into which they fit?

There is also an encouraging growth of interest in social trends. Since the society is the framework within which people's life styles develop, any changes in the society have their impact on life styles and, pragmatically, on markets. We are in a period of rapid change in which there is a lessening of the hold of traditional values and traditional behaviour. We saw this very clearly a few years ago in our studies of working class women, a type we had studied for many years. Suddenly, this woman was breaking out of her long-traditional role centered in home, husband and children and was becoming more independent as a person, and with new expectations as to what a woman could be and do. It is interesting to note that this change which we saw in our studies of working-class women was more broadly and more articulately expressed in the "woman's lib" movement. The women we studied generally rejected the publicity of women's lib but were accepting many of the values in their own lives.

Understanding these social trends and their impact on life style will probably become more important to research and to the agencies and advertisers who must anticipate the changes. However, research must not only explore social change but also constantly study its impact on life style and value systems. At the same time, we must study the linkage between these changes and the effects of advertising communication. The advertiser must talk to his customers in a meaningful way, but with rapid social change, he is always faced with a moving target and what may be effective communication today may be obsolete tomorrow.

I want now to give my thoughts about what needs to be done if we are to improve attitude research and make it a more effective tool for our society. Again, I state that I'm taking the broadest view of attitude research as being any research in which we ask people questions about their internal feelings or attitudes. This takes in a very large proportion of consumer research but excludes objectively verifiable or observable behaviour.

To make progress, we must do several things:

1. We must develop working hypotheses about how attitudes are formed or influenced. This should not be grandi-

8

ose theories beyond our capabilities of testing, but
should give help and direction for testing the theories in the real world of people as they are. For
example, we know that some people have negative attitudes toward "big business." In our research, we have
found that these negative attitudes or biases may ex-
tend to specific companies. We do not know much
about the specific elements in one's life situation
which affects his biases with respect to specific companies. We know even less what effect corporate advertising campaigns have on these biases or why.

2. We must test these working hypotheses again and again
    to learn the limits of their validity. Think of the
    way a pharmaceutical house develops a new drug. Some
    one has a theory based on observation or deduction, a
    drug is developed and tried on animals. Finally, it
    is tested carefully on small samples of patients.
    Eventually, it is released with elaborate statements
    of when to use it, what it will do, what are possible
    side effects, etc. In our field and applications we
    try a hypothesis once, and if it doesn't work the
    first time we discard it. We never repeat our experi-
    ments or even make public resports of either success
    or failure.

    In testing, we must rely more on intensive digging be-
    low the surface to try to understand the response to a
    question or the motivations of an action and not just
    rely on samples of superficial information. We must
    dig below the numbers to understand why they came
    about. Incidentally, in cooperation with a number of
    agencies and advertisers, we are starting a continuing
    study in which we will try to understand our respon-
    dents thoroughly and can test questions dealing with
    the subjective elements and biases and their influence
    on behaviour. This will be our method or model for
    getting below the numbers. This development of a pub-
    lic body of knowledge will require the wide under-
    standing of concepts and theories to be tested. Of-
    ten results of past studies no longer of proprietary
    value can be used for this testing. But without hypo-
    thesis, we don't know what to look for in the accumu-
    lated data or how to use it.

3. We must develop a public body of knowledge upon which
    we can build. Similar studies are repeated over and
    over again by different companies or agencies and the
    results are considered proprietary and are filed and
    often forgotten. The volume of studies conducted over

9

the years by any large company or agency is tremendous, yet it is not organized into a body of knowledge
upon which the studies can build. Each study is a
separate entity almost as though a doctor treated each
patient for a completely new and unique case.

4. We must constantly work at linking results of the
   studies growing out of the hypotheses to practical applications. Since we are dealing with the workings of
   the mind which we cannot examine directly, we must
   find the linkage of these results to the external behaviors. Just as in medicine, the theory of bacteria
   carrying infection in operations led to aseptic procedures and prevention of post-operative infections.

Remember, we are dealing with mental processes which
enable the organism to respond to the chaos of sensory input.
The tendency is to go off into philosophical constructs and
theories which are at best only partially true and often are
untestable in real life. As one of the top advertising leaders
once said: "I believe half my advertising does not work, but I
don't know which half."

With so much dependent on our studies of attitudes and
their formation, it is time we began to understand them better.

REFERENCES

1. Land, Edwin H. "Our Polar Partnership with the World
   Around Us," Harvard Magazine, January-February 1978.

2. Murrary, Thomas. In Advertising Age (February 27, 1978),
   p. 51.

3. Plummer, Joe. Life Style Applications to Media. Presented
   at a meeting of the Association of National Advertisers,
   March 1978.

4. Roethlisberger, F.J. The Elusive Phenomena, Harvard University Press, 1978.

5. Smith, Adam. Powers of Mind, Random House, 1975.

IDENTIFYING AND MEASURING TRENDS

IN CONSUMER OPINIONS/SOCIAL VALUES

Florence Skelly, Yankelovich, Skelly & White

Over the past eight years, my firm has been measuring and tracking social values via Monitor, a multi-sponsor research service for consumer marketers. I would like to share with you some of the principles for conducting such trend research which have emerged from the eight years we have under our belts.

Before discussing general principles, let me address a prior issue, namely, why bother to identify and track social values? Why should this be of interest to marketers?

We've learned that more and more marketers are finding it necessary to make both strategic and tactical decisions based on data at three levels of specificity:

-- First, and most specific: feedback on the performance of their own brands.

-- Second, and still fairly specific: feedback on the performance of the total product class in which they operate. Is it growing? What is the competitive climate? What new needs are emerging? How are they being served? Etc.?

-- Third, and broadest in scope, feedback on what is happening in the consumer climate in general. For example: what demographic shifts are being projected and do these matter to the business? What microeconomic changes are being forecast and how will these impact? Of increasing importance since the 1960's at this general feedback level -- has been a concern with the direction of social values in the United States and how these could affect consumer thinking and behavior.

Marketers -- like the rest of us -- are aware of the "winds of change" in life goals, in beliefs about what is success, the good life, right and wrong, etc. They hear it from their kids -- their wives. They read, go to the movies, watch TV. Many worry about what the changes mean for their product classes. For example:...a marketer of analgesics hears his kids talking about natural things, e.g., the natural life, natural food, natural cures, etc. -- and worries about whether they will use his product...a marketer of life insurance worries about what changing ideas about marriage and the family mean for personal life insurance...a foundation garment marketer worries about whether new goals for women means an end to bras and girdles.

Some marketers -- on the other hand -- decide that the changes in values that they see in their close circles are unique to them, a result of faulty upbringing or genes -- and deny that changes are really happening. They ignore the changes.

Systematically-collected reliable social value trend measurements can:

-- avoid under- or over-reaction by marketers.

-- insure that the marketer is not working with a set of assumption about values -- usually described as "the human condition" -- that are out of sync with the times and with his market.

-- provide a picture of the kinds of new life values that are emerging so that long-term strategic planning can take these into account.

-- describe current beliefs, goals, concerns so that near-term marketing action can be sharpened.

Monitor now has some 90 clients. Some are using this type of environmental tracking more than others. Once the potential power of the tool is experienced, you have a dedicated convert.

Enough of the why of social values tracking. Now for a few words about the how.

IDENTIFYING TRENDS

I think you would agree that it is no trick to identify an emerging value when it is part of the lives of a substantial portion of the people -- in other words, if, let us say, 40% of the population share a new value, it's nice to pin down the precise statistic, but it is no trick. The hard part -- the real challenge to any tracking system -- is to start tracking when emerging values are actually in an embryonic state so that you can really signal new developments before everybody from Time Magazine knows about it.

12

I'd like to share with you five things that we've learned in the process of trying to do exactly that. First, there is a real need to go beyond statistical modeling, and to crystalize and articulate a process model for how social change spreads. There should, for example, be an understanding of how filtration patterns within populations have moved and can move. Which groups are precursors? How are new values articulated and disseminated within a population? Also, there is a need to get a clear understanding of what we have called the process of transformation. If members of a fringe group are wearing very long hair -- (men, I mean) -- and long beards, transformation can be seen when a Mid-west business executive gets sideburns and longer hair. You don't have to see identical evidence when you are looking for spread of something which starts in fringe group. I have used a physical manifestation just to make the point. Similarly, a coherent, articulated set of values from a fringe group or an outside avant-garde group, very often is transformed -- it is toned down, it is tempered -- when it is picked up by the population at large. The best source for working out a process model usually is intensive analysis of history and synthesis of cases plus a lot of social theory.

Second: assume and make peace with the idea that not everything that emerges for your consideration as an embryonic value will actually grow and spread. You're going to be measuring some duds, things that never get off the ground. We have tried to err on the side of over-kill in order to insure completeness. Be prepared that some values are articulated by some very small fringe groups and never go anywhere; they do not have the power, the strength or the fortitude to actually sweep through the country and become anything that is worthy of serious consideration by a marketer.

The third point: focus your most intensive primary research on some key sources once you have articulated the process model. For example, from the point of view of population sub-groups -- college youth, blacks, two-earner households, the gay movement -- right now are very good mines to explore for articulation of new life values. Understanding the flow of change from one geographic area to another is also useful. The Far West and the Pacific Northwest have at the present time, a certain precursor character and it is extremely useful to do primary research in communities there, looking for emergence and articulation of values that are not found in the rest of the country -- at least at the moment. Something that we've learned that might interest you is that another source for intensive primary work (aside from geographic regions and population sub-groups) is our popular culture. Strangely enough, music, i.e., pop music has in themes, modes, and tone, been ahead of all the other cultural media in suggesting values

13

worth further study. The Beatles articulated, it later turns out, some of the things that we tracked in Monitor. When Dylan changed to soft and sweet, it signaled something. I know there have been some doctoral theses written about the role of popular music as a leading edge medium, more so than films, TV, theater.

Fourth: as possible new values emerge from these initial efforts, you have to really be sure that you have unearthed a possible basic value shift -- not a fad, which we have called only a manifestation of a new value. If it is a basic value change, there will be manifestations in many aspects of life -- not only in one. For example, let me give you the case of naturalism. In the 1960's, we saw an anti-technology thrust arise, linked to anti-materialism. Anti-technology went hand in glove with the extolling of naturalism as a new theme or a new social value. You saw it everywhere. In the universities, there were some serious questions about the rigors of the scientific method; physicists started to write papers talking about how this or that model worked but they didn't like the way it felt -- a sort of mystical approach. We saw in in natural food, natural ingredients, the natural look, natural decor -- there were a host of ways in which new commitment to naturalism was being expressed, which made it more than a temporary fad. If we had only seen an isolated interest in "natural" food, it would not have had the far reaching character to warrant its designation as a social value change.

The fifth and last point: work to trace the source of the value shift. Value shifts, historically, are unlikely to emerge just out of the blue; I mean you don't wake up one morning and say, "Hey, I have a new set of values." In the case of naturalism, it was an outgrowth of the anti-materialism of college youth in the 1960's. In turn, the anti-materialism was also something that many social scientists had anticipated once a psychology of affluence becomes part of any culture. In other words, review of social theory suggested that there were stimuli and origins of the new values that go beyond the influence of a strong entertainment personality or a strong political figure. This is not to say that charismatic spokespeople can't change or modify social values -- but usually they don't. What happens is that such personalities articulate and tap into some of the changes that are occurring; they may speed up the process of change, but very rarely do basic social or life values shift from just a single person's impact, however profound, however moving.

Those are five principles that have been emerging from our work in identifying social change.

14

I thought you might be interested in what we've learned about measuring abstractions such as changing values. I will move rather rapidly now because I don't think anything I'm saying here is terribly brilliant or new, but maybe putting it together in one place will be helpful.

First, as you might expect, one item is not enough. We have not found a way for measuring "Blurring of the Sexes," for example by a nice simple item such as "Do you feel that you would like to see the sexes blurred...very much, somewhat or hardly at all." It's not that such a possibility wouldn't make life a lot easier for everybody, but it doesn't work. One item is simply not enough. You need a battery of items to be sure that what you're measuring is more than a facile response to an idea that you yourself have articulated.

Second, the battery of items should not be identical in scale design, nor redundant in content, nor positioned sequentially in your questionnaire.

You have to avoid patterned responses, if you are to get valid measures of abstractions such as life values. This is nothing new; all the psychological tests that have survived follow this principle.

Third: in item design, we have found that self-referent items work a lot better than projectives. With the diversity in our population, a real problem with projectives is that people think they are answering for what they understand about the times, rather than for themselves, when it comes to social values. If you project a new value, and try to find out whether the person is in agreement with it, very often you will find, if you do reinterviewing, that the reason that he or she answered positively was not because the value was in line with the respondent's beliefs and feelings but rather because of awareness that more and more people support the value. We have found on some of these issues, that projectives give you an idea of how many people are following Time Magazine and television.

Fourth: this is a principle of value measurement which made life harder for us, it is important, nonetheless. Avoid in your item development, the use of capsule, current phrases even if they are very clear and descriptive. It would have been easier for us in tracking the trend "away from self-improvement" to use the phrase, "Let it be;" the Beatles were big at that time. Phrases like "Tell it like it is," very often capture the essence of a new value. ("Tell it like it is" is a

15

capsule description of anty-hypocrisy.) Don't use such phrases. A certain part of your population will know exactly what you're talking about when you use such a phrase. These are the people who are at the forefront of the new values. For a sizeable proportion of the population (which you also want to be looking at because you want to find out if a new value is reaching non-precursor groups) these such phrases have a meaning beyond their content. If the phrase is associated with a particular group -- racial, fringe, etc. -- you can find that you are measuring attitudes toward the group rather than toward content.

Five: In writing items, avoid use of current-people examples. There is a real temptation to use Joe Namath, Jane Fonda, Archie Bunker, for example, as prototypes of certain values because they may make the point extremely well. Such items, however, will not track well. Take Mia Farrow, for example. She represented a commitment to mysticism in 1966, when we were first starting some of our development work. And, the item using her as an example worked well. But, such an item today would be meaningless.

Six: This point is a little subtle. Be careful to differentiate social change from personality traits. One of the concepts we had trouble with along these lines was the trend away from system and order in the sense of rejection of certain aspects of the Protestant Ethic life style, i.e., commitment to a settled, orderly planned life. It's all too easy to find that what you're tracking is not a change in belief about the good or evil of a totally ad hoc life style versus the systematic one. You'll find yourself really measuring compulsivity, which is a -- shall we say -- a personality characteristic, which has absolutely nothing to do with social change.

Seven: We have found a powerful need for context setting in questionnaire design. In psychological testing, context setting is not used. In our survey work for tracking social change, however, we found that we had to periodically remind the respondent of our purpose. This can be done in a sentence or two; you don't have to elaborate or to bare your soul. But some of the material you get into is so weird in their minds (interesting, yes, but puzzling also) -- that you have to continue to set the context or you will be talking to somebody who is answering your questions while worrying about your purposes.

Eight, and last: We learned through extensive statistical analysis of our early work that items can be framed in either the positive or negative expressions of a value or belief -- and that you don't have to do both ritualistically. We found a very high correlation between responses to the positive and

16

negative statements. This free-ups the item writer to choose the mode that makes the most sense, the item that sounds the best and is most conversational.

Those are some of the principles that we have learned from the social value tracking research that was initiated in the late 1960's. We are continuing to learn as the Monitor program continues, and I look forward to hearing the other speakers and learning from their experiences.

PREDICTING ATTITUDE TRENDS

James A. Davis
Harvard University

This paper shows how the NORC[1] General Social Surveys
(GSS) can be used to study the development of public opinion
trends. Sponsored by the National Science Foundation, the GSS
is an annual survey of English-speaking adults in the United
States. The first section of the paper provides some background on the survey and the second describes some opinion
trends which have been observed during the years since the survey's inception in 1972.

BACKGROUND ON THE GSS

The survey is conducted in March of each year by means of
personal interviews with a sample representative of the English
speaking adults in the continental United States. The spon-
sorship of the National Science Foundation contributes three
unique features to the survey.

First of all, it is totally eclectic, and that's why it's
called the General Social Survey. We decided to develop an instrument that would be of interest to a wide variety of social
scientists so we carried out a poll. We contacted the editors
of journals, the members of numerous organizations, my friends,
NORC staff, etc., and gave them a list of potential survey
items to rate. Anything that got six ticks got in. Whereupon,
in true sociological fashion, I developed a recursive model of
the whole thing it turned out that it consists of: (1) personal
background characteristics, including stratification variables
-- what did Daddy do for a living, where did you grow up, were
you rich, were you poor, how far did you go in school, and so
forth; (2) many attitude and opinion items (I'll be talking a
little bit about them later); (3) quite a few measures of
morale, trust confidence, loathing and the like; and, (4) not
an awful lot directly relevant to consuming this or that. It
is totally eclectic -- a little bit of everything. Further,
information on the survey can be obtained by writing to NORC.

Second, it is designed as a replication study. Virtually
every item was taken from a previous national sample of some
sort, which meant that from the very beginning we could look at
change. Most of the original items come from NORC studies,

---

[1]National Opinion Research Center, 6030 South Ellis,
Chicago, IL 60637

Michigan studies -- particularly the election series, Gallup, and Harris studies. Many items are replicated each year although some are on a rotation system. It was designed in a cute way -- actually by Dudley Duncan -- so that within any three years you could get the zero order correlation between any two items that keep reappearing.

The third unique feature of it is sort of an organizational feature. It's designed to be put in the public domain immediately. NORC has no particular program for analyzing it. We put GSS in the public domain immediately -- we shoot for July 1 of each year and -- here's the hard sales pitch -- we have a new feature, a cumulative tape of the entire series of surveys. The current (1972) to 1977) cumulative GSS tape is available for $50 from the Roper Public Opinion Research Center at Yale University, New Haven, Connecticut.

This cumulative feature is one that we didn't really anticipate but is of increasing value. As you repeat the items over and over and over again, cases pile up. We have now a total of about 9,000 and each year we'll ad about 1500 and we are getting to the point where we have, for example, enough people who have been mugged (130) to maybe have a look at them. Cases in very small cells pile up and, of course, larger cells pile up faster -- we now have about 1,000 blacks. As you know, studies of the black population are very difficult to do in national surveys because you don't get enough of them. I will not tell you how few counties our rural section blacks are coming out of -- but we do have over a thousand cases in the cumulative file.

These then are the three major features of the study -- it's eclectic; it involves replication, both each year and replication, both each year and replicaton of previous base line items; and, it is designed to be put into the public domain quickly and cheaply.

THE STUDY OF CATEGORICAL DATA OVER TIME

Some Background on Events

How much, if any, change have we detected during the first six years of the survey? The period of 1972 to 1977 is not a long time as social change goes -- but it was quite a wild time and in working this up I went off to the Library and looked up the events of the period. We first went in the field in March of 1972 and on February 21 -- just before GSS-1972 went into the field, Nixon arrived in Peking -- it was the height of the Nixon presidency.

Shortly after we came out of the field, there was the Watergate break-in (June 17) and the Supreme Court ruling against capital punishment (June 25). In August of 1972 we started to get out of Viet Nam, in the Fall Nixon won, on December 18 Nixon ordered the Christmas bombing. Early in 1973 (January 22) we had the Supreme Court ruling on abortion -- I want to come back to that -- the Viet Nam settlement (January 27), Watergate really began just before GSS-1973 went into the field. Then came Fall 1973. We had the Arab-Israeli war, the oil embargo, the Saturday night massacre, the fuel crisis, the Ford pardon of Nixon, and the collapse of South Viet Nam. The last completed General Social Survey (GSS-1977) went into the field a couple of weeks after Carter was inaugerated. Six years is not a long time but, to the extent that attitudes and opinions are influenced by the sort of things that you see on the evening news, it was quite a wild time. We also had stagflation -- with consequences I'll turn to in a minute.

Now, during this period we replicated several hundred items. There are about 450 mnemonics in the whole thing and, for present purposes, I want to talk about 205 questions that were asked four or more times. Some questions have only been asked three times. For example, our sex role and sex items are really going to come up for their fourth shot right now -- so we don't have much on change there. Therefore, I will talk about the 205 items that were replicated four to six times in the period.

A Word on Statistics

First of all, it's necessary to discuss some statistics. If you run to your neighborhood library and check out your handy book on time series analysis and Box-Jenkins, and all that, you will find that you can do some terribly exciting things with time-trend studies as soon as you get, say, 50 or 60 points. However, for somebody sitting there with at the most 6 time points, even though each of them cost about $250,000, the classical textbook approaches to time series analysis are not all that revealing. Therefore, we had to forge our own hand-to-mouth ways of ginning out statistical results. Table 1 presents the general idea of how we work.

You would not think that doing regression with 3 or 4 time points would be a morally acceptable way to proceed, except that you have to remember that each of them is based on 1500 cases (call it 750 what with clustering in the sample design). Therefore, if one of our years is 20 points out of line, that means an awful lot more than if case #0375 is way out of line. What we do is try to capitalize on the principle -- it's a fitting procedure. We try to fit the data with the least ac-

20

TABLE 1

FITTING VARIOUS TREND HYPOTHESES TO SETS OF PROPORTIONS

Example of a constant trend for the proportion reporting
"own health is excellent."

1972	1973	1974	1975	1976	1977	
.300	.319	.328	.324	.313	.318	
.317	.317	.317	.317	.317	.317	= pooled p
-.017	+.002	+.011	+.007	-.004	+.001	Chi Sq=1.7 prob=.883

Example of a linear declining trend for the proportion
reporting "too much defense spending."

1972	1973	1974	1975	1976	1977	
NA	.383	.310	.310	.272	.229	
--	.296	.296	.296	.296	.296	= pooled p
	+.087	+.014	+.014	-.024	-.067	Chi Sq=47.4 prob=.001
--	.370	.336	.301	.226	.232	=regression line
	.013	-.026	+.009	+.046	-.003	Chi Sq=3.3 prob=.349

47.3 - 3.3 = 44.3, prob = .001

Example of no trend with the proportion reporting
own happiness as "very happy."

1972	1973	1974	1975	1976	1977	
.303	.359	.379	.329	.341	.348	
.342	.342	.342	.342	.342	.342	= pooled p
-.039	+.017	+.037	-.013	-.001	+.006	Chi Sq=23.5 prob=.001
.334	.338	.348	.345	.349	.352	= regression line
-.031	+.021	+.031	-.016	-.008	-.004	Chi Sq=21.4 prob=.001

23.5 - 21.4 = 2.1, prob = .144

21

tion possible and the least action possible is nothing happening.

As an example, let's take the item "How's your own health -- excellent, good, fair, poor?" Table 1 shows the proportion saying their health is excellent, and I, of course, chose it because it illustrates the point neatly. We see the proportion "excellent" zooms from 30, to 32, to 31, to 32 -- that is, it just sits there. As a statistical test for the constancy hypothesis, we pool the individual proportions to get a common proportion. Then we use a chi square test to see if they all come out like the common proportion, which, of course, they do have in Table 1 -- as things always do in the first classroom example you give out.

Now, of the 205 items, about half came out essentially constant. To me, that is the most interesting find of all. It means it is possible, year after year, to band together a couple hundred interviewers who never see each other, mail out some mimeographed stuff hoping everybody gets the same envelope at the same time, conduct interviews on a new sample, and get back answers that are pretty close to each other. I consider that very good news in terms of the technology of the profession. For, if all our items are changing, I would not assume we were a dynamic society, but that NORC does lousy field work and sampling. By the way, they are not chosen because they are supposed to change or not change, they are chosen to be interesting. The "own health" example is a fairly illustrative one.

Now if an item is changing -- that is, you can't fit it with a constant -- the next thing you do is see if you can place a straight line through it and improve your fit. For example, a linear declining trend is shown in the middle of Table 1. It is part of a package of ten items about spending on national problems -- "do you think we're spending too much, to little, or about right on solving the problem?"

The example shows the proportion of people saying we're spending too much on defense. It began in 1973 with about 38 percent and has declined steadily. Statistically, it has not just been sagging, it has been going down in a nice linear fashion so that when we place a regression line through it the chi square goes away. That is, we can explain all of that trend by fitting a straight line. Now of the 205 items -- remember I said half of them didn't change -- the remaining half divide evenly between those that really show a significant change and those that seem to be showing a change, but significance is borderline. Of the 48 items showing significant change, about half show this linear sort of pattern -- so about a quarter of all the items we measured showed some sort of

22

trend -- they're going up or they're going down throughout the period.

The last possibility is something that is changing around but not going in any direction consistently. This pattern is demonstrated in the bottom of Table 1. The Table shows the proportions rating one's own happiness as very, as opposed to pretty, or not too happy. (Those of you who are into the happiness measurement business know that happiness wordings are very sensitive to the middle category. This is the Michigan -- NORC happiness, not Gallup happiness.) Happiness shows statistically significant fluctuation but a linear fit does not help at all -- that is, it is fluctuating -- going up, down more than a chance would account -- but with no particular direction. Seventeen of our items show that pattern.

What this all has to do with prediction is the simple notion that if things are fluctuating in a trendless fashion, it's mighty hard to predict them -- but if there is constancy or sort of a line, at least you can make a reasoned guess about what's going to happen next year. But enough of the statistical legerdemain -- let's move on to the substantive findings.[2]

SOME TRENDS IN THE GSS DATA

The items that show the largest amount of change can be roughly grouped into four categories -- Economic, Political Identification, National Priorities, and Confidence in Leaders and Institutions, Economic Data.

Change in Economic Trends

The largest change in the Economic Data was the increase in nominal family income. At first I thought it was a problem with the sampling, but since occupational level, education, and so forth, are not changing at all, and since it comes out exactly the same as the current population survey, I concluded the strongest single trend is the increasing median nominal family income in the population. This, of course, is a generally known fact.

What is less obvious is what folks make of it. Here, as you might expect, the subjective reading is somewhat different. There are three subjective financial items that bear on this issue. One item is the proportion of people saying that their financial situation is getting better or worse. The proportion

---

[2]For a further explanation of the procedure, see James A. Davis, "Studying Categorical Data Over Time," Social Science Research, 1978.

23

saying, "Yes, things are better," went <u>down</u> steadily throughout this period 1972 to 1977 and proportion "worse" went up steadily.

A second item is "How is your income compared to everyone else?" The proportion saying their own is below average went up steadily. Every year a greater proportion of the American population felt it was below average. The proportion above average didn't change much. Thus, people thought things were getting worse -- fewer people thought things were getting better -- more people thought that they were in the bottom of the pile. However, the item on "satisfaction" with income did not change at all. This finding is now becoming notorious in the social indicator field -- satisfaction items cannot be moved -- they are rocks, next to which family composition is a volatile projective item.

So our big change in terms of size of the effect is increased apparent income, decreased feeling of income improvement -- but no great change in income satisfaction. This is worth remembering because I don't think we can explain changes in other things through increasing dissatisfaction if dissatisfaction is not increasing. People clearly feel they are not doing as well but this has not yet been turned into an "Oh my God," sort of personal feeling.

Change in Political Identification Items

The second batch of items showing sharp changes can be roughly termed liberal vs. conservative items. This doesn't mean that each of them correlates with our item on self-rated liberalism or conservatism, but they are the sort of things that researchers tend to think of as liberal or conservative. Is there a conservative trend? We get a mixed reading. We get very strong increases on three "conservative" items - two of them are Gallup items. "The courts around here are not harsh enough" takes off like a rocket. Capital punishment is increasingly popular in the American population, which is rather interesting. It's one of the few items with a long-term U-shaped trend. Favorability toward capital punishment went down in the 1960's and it is now going up at a fairly fast rate, despite the Supreme Court ruling limiting capital punishment. This is a case where opinion does not follow the courts. The last conservative item is one we made up, an anti-communism question. It turned out -- although this is the political question that has driven American society for forty years -- to our knowledge nobody ever asked folks if they are for or against communism -- they knew the answer. Well, we asked them. They are not wild about communism, I can assure you, although there are some 30 people each year who says it's a wonderful form of government. "Communism is the worst form of government" is one of our big increasers throughout the period, which is rather interesting because the years 1952 to 1977 appear to be a period of defusing of U.S.-Russian confrontations.

Now, on the "liberal" side, we have a decreasing ideal family size. The number of people wanting large families has gone down steadily throughout the period, as it has for a long time. Attitudes toward racial marriages and the possibility of voting for a black for President have become more liberal. One of the more interesting of the liberal trends is the abortion question. We have an abortion battery of about six items and what happened was, after the Supreme Court decision, they all went up -- and then just stayed frozen ever since -- the most beautiful step function you ever saw in your life. Each went up about five or six percent and there have been virtually no changes since a month after the Supreme Court decision. Now, of course, you could have a lot of individual oscillation around this mean, but the level has not changed at all.

It's very hard, then, since we have both liberal and conservative items increasing for me to say there either is a general liberal or conservative trend.

Change in National Priorities Items

The questions on spending priorities are of the "Goldilocks" type -- we should be spending more, the spending is about right, or we should be spending less. For instance, in 1973, 65 percent said we were spending too little on the crime problem and only 10 percent said we were spending too much. In 1973, the top priorities were crime, drugs, health and the environment. Defense, the space program, were not doing so well, and both welfare and foreign aid were downright unpopular.

During the period of 1972 to 1977 the striking shift was an increase in favorability toward defense spending. The others remained in about the same rank order and the distance among them has become compressed.

Change in Confidence Items

Some of the most volatile items were those which asked about confidence in leaders and institutions. First, however, I would like to point out that two of these items, confidence in the courts and confidence in the press, did not change at all during this period. I like that because it indicates that what changes we do find are not totally an artifact of sampling or interviewing -- if a couple of the items do not change then you have to pay some attention to what is going on with the others.

Two of the greatest changes were confidence in Congress and confidence in the Executive Branch. This, of course, is a reflection of the public's response to the events of Watergate -- obvious -- except what is not so obvious is that Congress took exactly the same beating as the White House.

In the middle were the ratings for medicine, science, education, the military, the clergy, business and labor. Each had a complicated pattern. There were strongly significant changes -- lots of variables -- but each ended up where it began. These items showed great variation, but practically nothing in the way of trends over the years 1972 to 1977.

CONCLUSION

My comments have just highlighted the patterns of change and stability observed in the NORC General Social Surveys. A more detailed report on the survey results is available from NORC, and, of course, the cumulative tape can be obtained from the Roper Center at Yale University.

SEARCHING FOR OPINION TRENDS IN FOREIGN POLICY

Bernard Roshco, U. S. Department of State

INTRODUCTION

Recently, I asked a friend: What lesson had he learned from the role that public-opinion data had played in the controversy over the Panama Canal treaties? Keep in mind that I was inquiring about a political confrontation during which polls were getting more publicity than at any time since the last Presidential election. It was a situation in which there was intensive interaction between the 3 P's of public life: the press, the polls, and the policy-makers. My friend's reply was that he'd been most impressed by the media's capacity to "market marginals."

I think he has a point. Two of the networks have their own polling units, NBC and CBS. Each did two polls on Panama. The questions were similar but, of course, each network employed different wording. Each network's marginals were broadcast on its own evening news show. Then the media-market multiplier took over: the marginals were repeated on network radio the next morning and appeared in some of the same day's papers. I suppose AP and UPI picked them up and spread them still further.

Television's in-house pollsters have a bigger audience for their marginals than the other media. Still, by the time the first of the Panama treaties came to a vote, everybody who was anybody in polling circles appears to have weighed in with some questions.

Yankelovich, Skelly and White, whose data found its national audience in TIME magazine. The Associated Press retained Chilton Research for a one-shot poll. Gallup, Harris, Roper -- each had his own questions, each repeated them several times, with some variant wording in the course of the repetitions.

Besides the national polls, there were regional polls, such as Mervin Field in California, who asked Panama questions at least twice. Also, a one-shot from the Iowa Poll and one from GMA Research covering the State of Washington. Other pollsters also produced data, such as Robert Teetor and Roger Seasonwein and, as you might expect, Pat Caddell. This partial listing should give you an idea of the plethora of available numbers.

27

The record for running the longest contemporary trend probably goes to Opinion Research Corporation, which went into the field for the first time in June 1975. It went back three more times, most recently in February 1978. Along the way, it dropped some questions and introduced others.

Despite the ORC coverage, the record for the earliest polling ever done on Panama goes to Gallup, who just edges out the Minnesota Poll on that score. They both asked questions in 1964, after the riots erupted in Panama that started the whole process of negotiating a new treaty.

Unfortunately for me, I had no questions to call my very own. Or, perhaps, fortunately, since I have had no stake in anybody's data. I ought to explain that the State Department does not commission any polls of its own. We beg, borrow, and buy marginals, wheedle demographics, coax out crosstabs from other people's computers, and then stare at the results in search of meanings.

As a consequence of having to look at everybody else's data, I do have a cautionary tale to tell this morning, a profile in the political uses of polling data. I have a report to offer on the inadequacy of public-affairs polling, and on the frequent failure of reporters to take a reasonably close look at the poll data they are reporting.

Given all the available data, you may wonder why I titled this talk, "searching" for trends. There appear to have been enough trends to satisfy the hungriest number-cruncher.

That is exactly the problem. In the course of the Panama controversy, Washington politicians were searching for trends. There were votes to be won and lost back home, and Congress wanted to know what was on the public's mind. It was a seller's market for trends; the problem was, there wasn't a clear-cut, politically sure and safe trend to be found.

SEARCHING FOR TRENDS

In September of 1977, one of the powers of the Senate, Senator Robert Byrd of West Virginia, the majority leader, took cognizance of the most highly publicized poll result at the time -- the 78 percent of a national sample who reportedly opposed "giving away" the Panama Canal. Senator Byrd set the base point for the trend that would count most with the Senate when he announced that the treaties could not be passed unless public opinion could be moved away from such overwhelming opposition.

28

Senator Jesse Helm of North Carolina, a leading opponent of the treaties, had been particularly effective in publicizing that number. The press picked it up from him and then from each other -- and soon it was enshrined as accepted wisdom.

To my knowledge, no newsperson ever reported the question on which that marginal was based. It was, "Do you favor the United States continuing its ownership and control of the Panama Canal, or do you favor turning ownership and control of the Panama Canal over to the Republic of Panama?" The surface objectivity of this question is a model of disingenuousness. It's also an excellent example of why it's so hard to frame questions on foreign-policy issues that result in informative answers.

In any event, I think it's ironic that 78 percent became the accepted level of opposition to the treaties as the Senate got ready to debate the treaties. When you're that far down, you have no place to go but up. Of course, just how far public opinion actually moved in the direction pf approval became the bone of political contention.

The story of the Panama polls is a case history of the three conditions that are the bane of seriously intentioned public-affairs polling, particularly on foreign policy. Leo Bogart once summarize them as: (1) ignorance of the facts; (2) misunderstanding of the issues; (3) inability to visualize consequences.

In his book on public affairs and public opinion, Silent Politics, Bogart wrote: "Public opinion is commonly measured for and against various causes, with the undecided as the residue. Often it may be more revealing to measure the degree of apathy, indecision, or conflict on the part of the great majority and consider the opinionated as the residue. The first question a pollster should ask is: 'Have you though about this at all? Do you have an opinion?'"

I can think of no better text to serve as a starting point for a trend analysis of the apathetic, uninformed, and indecisive respondents whose answers have played so large a role in developing the data bank of public opinion on the Panama treaties.

I begin by reporting a question that was asked only once. Not only was it never repeated, but the fact it had been asked was never, to my knowledge, reported in the press. Consequently, the responses were never publicized.

In June 1975, Opinion Research Corporation conducted a na-

29

tional poll based on a sample of 1,021 for a Washington-based client named the American Council for World Freedom. That poll asked nine questions on Panama, and I'm quoting from the Council's press release. So the failure to publicize the data I am about to present was not a matter of deliberate concealment, but it was a journalistic oversight. In June 1975, the press did not think the Panama treaty negotiations were very newsworthy.

In any event, the first question asks, who owns the Panama Canal? You may think this is analogous to asking who's buried in Grant's Tomb, but the data prove you wrong. The question: "As you may know, the Panama Canal is the waterway in Central America that connects the Atlantic and Pacific Oceans. As far as you know, what country owns the Panama Canal and the Canal Zone surrounding it?"

The plurality response was: Don't Know, 44 percent; the next highest response was, United States, 35 percent; then Panama, 14 percent; other responses totaled seven percent, including Arabs, Israel, Cuba, Communists, and several who thought it was jointly owned by the United States and Panama.

We have here our first trend benchmark: two-thirds of the American public apparently didn't know who controls the Panama Canal as of June 1975.

Next, the sample was asked if it was aware of any treaty negotiations -- back in June 1975, mind you. The question: "The United States secured full ownership and control of the Canal Zone by way of a treaty signed with the Republic of Panama in 1903. How much, if anything, have you heard or read about the possiblity of negotiations on a new Panama Canal Treaty -- a great deal, a fair amount, very little, or nothing at all?"

Let us overlook the error in the wording -- the negotiation was not merely a possibility but an actuality that had been under way for 11 years under Presidents from both parties, facts that might certainly have influenced the uninformed in their responses to subsequent questions. Anyhow, those who claimed to have "heard or read" a "great deal" were five percent and those who said a "fair amount" came to 13 percent. Those who answered "very little" came to 42 percent, and "nothing at all" was the answer of 38 percent, supplemented by two percent who answered "don't know."

Another benchmark: 82 percent admit they are ignorant the Panama Canal is an issue. I am skeptical that as many as 18 percent really had some awareness of the negotiations. Be that as it may, we know the uninformed are a clear-cut majority. So far, the interviewer has told them the United States actually owns the Canal and the Canal Zone, but they have not been informed that negotiations are actually under way, let alone that they have been going on since 1964.

Then, this question comes out of the blue: "Do you favor the United States continuing its ownership and control of the Panama Canal, or do you favor turning ownership and control of the Panama Canal over to the Republic of Panama?"

In this bald context, 12 percent said they'd turn over the Canal to Panama. Unfortunately, we are not told the demographics of this group, nor how many of them knew the facts about ownership nor how informed about negotiations they had claimed to be. Contrasted with this 12 percent is 22 percent who answered "don't know" and 66 percent who said the United States should hold on to the canal.

Then there is a sequence of questions asking for opinion on whether Panama could run the canal and whether Panamanian ownership of the canal would hurt U.S. security and damage the U.S. economy. That trio of queries was introduced this way: "The population of the Republic of Panama is 1.6 million people -- about as many as live in Atlanta, Georgia. (Since the question was written in the spring of 1975, I believe the mention of Georgia was a coincidence, not a political statement.) Do you feel that a country the size of the Republic of Panama is or is not capable of operating and defending a major international waterway?"

To each of the three questions, the percentage of responses was virtually identical. Twenty-nine percent gave answers favorable to Panama, 50 or 51 percent gave answers unfavorable to Panama, and 20 or 21 percent answered, "don't know."

Then comes a question that offers an interesting sequel to the initial query, which had offered no rationale for turning over the canal. In this latter case, the question states: "As you may know, when a treaty is negotiated with a foreign country, the treaty has to be voted on by the U.S. Senate. If a treaty is negotiated turning over ownership and control of the Panama Canal to the Republic of Panama, do you think the U.S. Senate should approve or disapprove such a treaty?"

Again, the approving response was 29 percent. Disapproval was 48 percent, and no opinion was 23 percent.

As we review these questions, we see that this one poll produced its own internal trend: 12 percent gave outright ap-

31

proval to turning over the canal, right off the bat, without needing a further explanation. An additional 17 percent apparently would not find it too disturbing if the canal did wind up in Panamanian hands. We seem to have a scale of degrees of acquiescence, ranging from approval to acceptance.

This poll provided initial data for three trends: (1) basic knowledge about the canal; (2) awareness of negotiations; (3) attitudes toward a change in control.

The question of who owns the canal was never to be repeated. Eventually, Gallup would ask and repeat a trio of questions regarding basic provisions of the treaty and the utility of the canal. ORC would continue to ask its awareness question, as would others; therefore,the substantial increase of awareness is easily traced. Presumably, such awareness was accompanied in most cases by realization that the United States currently controls the canal, though it would be interesting to know how widely this bit of information has actually been assimilated since June 1975.

We still have to decide on the appropriate base figure for the most politically important trend of the three initiated for us by ORC. What was the initial division of opinion on placing control of the canal in Panamanian hands? Was it favored by 12 percent or by 29 percent?

The American Council for World Freedom believed the score was 12 percent for Panama to 66 percent against. The Council's lead on its new release for June 25, 1975 read: "By a margin of more than five to one, Americans favor continued U.S. ownership of the Panama Canal."

However, a paragraph at the bottom of the release's front page read: "Nearly half the people (48% vs. 29%) believe the U.S. Senate should disapprove rather than approve turning ownership of the canal over to Panama."

After June 1975, ORC went back into the field three more times: In April 1976; in May 1977; and in February 1978. New questions were introduced, and old ones were dropped, but two were retained from the initial survey: the one about attentiveness to negotiations and the bald query, "Do you favor the United States continuing its ownership and control of the Panama Canal, or do you favor turning ownership and control of the Panama Canal over to the Republic of Panama?"

By May 1977, the third time this question was asked, the proportion saying they wanted the United States to keep the canal had climbed to 78 percent from 66 percent in 1975 and 75 percent in 1976. Last May, only eight percent were telling ORC they favored Panamanian control.

The 29 percent who had responded in 1975 that the Senate should approve a treaty "turning over ownership and control of the Panama Canal to Panama" seemed to have disappeared, as definitively as the question that evoked their response.

Yet, their equivalent could still be found; but, you had to look for them in other people's polls. It turns out that the stability of pro-treaty responses (at approximately the 29 percent level) and of anti-treaty responses (at approximately the 53 percent level) -- across diverse questions put by different pollsters -- is one of the most interesting trends the data turned up.

For comparison with data from other polls that I am about to describe, keep in mind these figures from ORC's June 1975 poll: for treaty approval, 29 percent; against the treaty, 48 percent; no opinion, 23 percent.

Now compare this sequence of questions and responses:

Roper, January 1977: "Do you think the time has come for us to modify our Panama Canal Treaty or that we should insist on keeping the treaty as originally signed?" For modification, 24 percent; against, 53 percent; undecided, 23 percent.

Yankelovich, March 1977: "Do you favor or oppose giving the Panama Canal back to the Panamanians, even if we maintain our right to defend it?" For giving it back, 29 percent; for holding on to it, 53 percent; undecided, 18 percent.

Caddell, May 1977: "Do you think the United States should negotiate a treaty with Panama where, over a period of time, Panama will eventually own and run the Canal?" Should negotiate, 27 percent; should not negotiate, 51 percent; undecided, 22 percent.

ORC and Caddell asked their quite different questions and got their quite different results during the same month. But it was ORC's figure that became the publicized benchmark from which to measure the presumed trend. Getting this number accepted was not an unmixed advantage for anti-treaty forces. As a look at subsequent press coverage reveals, if you start an an extreme, subsequent data will almost inevitably create the impression that the trend is running against you.

Thus, on February 1, 1978, the New York _Times_ ran a story about the President's lobbying efforts in behalf of the treaties. One paragraph stated: "Last May, according to public opinion surveys conducted for the White House by pollster Patrick Caddell, an overwhelming 87 percent opposed the treaties. Today, that figure has been reduced to 55 percent, according to White House sources."

When I read that, my initial reaction was that a typo in the Times had reversed ORC's 78% to 87%. But that wouldn't account for crediting the figures to Caddell. I called Caddell's Washington office and was told they had no knowledge of the 87 percent figure. I queried the White House, and I was told they hadn't used that number.

However, marginals do have a way of finding new markets. The next day, the Christian Science Monitor ran a story under the byline of its distinguished and veteran Washington correspondent, Richard L. Strout. Mr. Strout had also prepared a story on the Administration's effort to turn public opinion around. Mr. Strout also reported a trend: "...popular opposition to yielding the canal has diminished markedly, according to opinion polls." Referring to the President's efforts, Mr. Strout wrote: "During his eight-month campaign, public opposition to the treaties has dropped from 87 percent to 55 percent..."

Eight months before February is May, the month ORC came out with its 78 percent figure. I was satisfied I had that end of the alleged trend figured out. What about the 55 percent? That figure turns up in a Caddell poll, conducted last October, which asked: "From what you do know about the treaty, do you generally favor or oppose it?" The opposed were 55 percent and it was favored by 30 percent. If that is the source of the number, I don't know why it was chosen, since more recent and somewhat more favorable numbers were available. (That should give pause to those who are quick to hypothesize conspiracy theories.)

For example, the White House could have cited the response to this CBS question, asked in January: "The Senate now has to debate the treaties that President Carter signed granting control of the Panama Canal to the Republic of Panama in the year 2000. Do you approve or disapprove of those treaties?"

Disapprove of the treaties, 51 percent; approve of them, 29 percent; no opinion, 20 percent.

In the meantime, a different sequence of questions resulted in a different alleged trend, which the Associated Press characterized late in February as an "erosion" of support.

34

This chapter of our search for a Panama treaty trend concerns NBC's polls.

NBC ran its first Panama poll last October. First, it asked: "Have you heard or read about the new treaty between the United States and the Republic of Panama regarding the Panama Canal?" Seventy-five percent answered "yes" and were asked: "The new treaty between the United States and Panama calls for the United States to turn over ownership of the canal to Panama at the end of this century. However, this treaty still has to be approved by the Senate. Do you favor or oppose approval of this treaty by the Senate?"

Opposition was 61 percent; support was 30 percent.

The questions were repeated in January, and the response had not changed at the level of statistical significance, let alone political significance. Instead of the 75 percent awareness in October, there was 77 percent in January. Opposition had shifted from 61 to 62 percent, and support from 30 to 28 percent. By January, however, treaty revision was in the news and NBC added this question:

"Would you favor or oppose approval of the Panama Canal treaty if an amendment were added, specifically giving the United States the right to intervene if the Canal is threatened by attack?' "

The question was asked of everyone, regardless of whether they expressed opposition or support in answering the previous question. The result was a complete turnaround: 65 percent favored a revised treaty, and 25 percent opposed it.

One response does not make a trend, of course, but there is a way of improvising a trend based on the follow-up question about the revised treaty. CBS had asked a comparable trio of questions in October. However, their similar follow-up was asked only of those who opposed the treaty on the initial question. Adding together those who supported the treaty on the initial question plus those who initially opposed it, but supported a revised treaty on the follow-up question, sums to 63 percent approval and 24 percent disapproval. On this basis, NBC's January findings were virtually identical to those of CBS in October.

This way of constructing a trend may lack something in methodological nicety. But a policy-maker is more concerned with whether it serves as a valid political indicator. That issue was beclouded in February, when NBC conducted its third nation-wide telephone poll on Panama. Again, it asked about

35

awareness of the treaties and got a positive response of 81 percent, up four percent from January. The aware were then asked:

"Would you favor or oppose approval of the Panama Canal treaty if an amendment were added, specifically giving the United States the right to intervene if the canal is threatened by attack and the right to send our warships to the head of the line in case of emergency?"

NBC had dropped its initial question and had gone straight to a revised version of the amended-treaty question. Predict for yourself what the response would be -- would support for opposition come out ahead?

The response was: in favor of such an amended treaty, 54 percent; opposed to it, 40 percent; and a surprisingly low "not sure" response of six percent.

The next day, the Associated Press carried the story, and characterized the data as showing an "erosion" of support for the treaty, having compared it with the 63 percent approval produced by the follow-up question in January.

Was there erosion? Was there actually a trend on which to base a comparison? My concluding remarks describe another sequence of data, and we will consider whether it could be characterized as a trend.

Early in October and again early in January, Gallup asked a sequence of questions. The introductory question was: "Have you heard or read about the debate over the Panama Canal treaty?" Then, a trio of questions testing knowledge was asked of those who claimed awareness, which was 74 percent in October and 81 percent in January.

First: "As far as you know, in what year is the Panama Canal to be turned over completely to the Republic of Panama by terms of the treaties?" The correct answer, any equivalent of the year 2000, was supplied by 35 percent of the aware in October but only by 25 percent in January.

Second: "As far as you know, will the United States have the right to defend the Panama Canal against third nation attack after Panama takes full control?" The correct answer is "yes", offered by 58 percent in October and 67 percent in January.

Third question: "To the best of your knowledge, how much do the biggest U.S. aircraft carriers and supertankers now use the Panama Canal -- a great deal, quite a lot, not very much or not at all?" The correct answer, "not at all," was provided by 19 percent in October and 30 percent in January. In October, six percent of the 74 percent of aware respondents got all three questions right. In January, a little less than 10 percent of the 81 percent of aware respondents got all three right.

All the respondents were asked this final question: The treaties would give Panama full control over the Panama Canal and the Canal Zone by the year 2000, but the United States would retain the right to defend the Canal against a third nation. Do you favor or oppose these treaties between the U.S. and Panama?"

In October, the opposition was 46 percent and support was 36 percent. In January, there was a turnaround: opposition was down to 37 percent and support was up to 43 percent.

However, let us not forget that ORC had all along been pursuing its own trend question. In February, it asked, for the fourth time, the same question originated in June 1975. The latest data showed hardly a change, let alone a turnaround. In fact, opposition to turning over the canal was greater than in 1975, though lower than in May, which produced the highly publicized 78 percent. This time opposition was 72 percent. Support for turning over control to Panama was 19 percent, up from the eight percent of May and the 12 percent of June 1975, but nothing like the recurrent 29 percent figure that ORC itself had first produced on the question it later dropped.

As we continue our search for a definitive trend, we come to one more twist in the road, where we meet a Lou Harris poll. About the same time ORC was fielding its February poll, Harris was in the field with Panama questions, his second time since September. Harris's February question was similar to his September question, but not an exact repetition.

In February, he asked: "Do you favor or oppose the U.S. Senate approving the proposed treaties with Panama on the Panama Canal?"

In September, he had asked: "As you know, President Carter asked the U.S. Senate to vote approval of a new treaty between the U.S. and Panama which will hand control of the Panama Canal back to Panama by the year 2000. Would you favor or oppose the U.S. Senate approving this treaty with Panama?"

Compared to September, opposition had declined and supporters and the undecided were both up. The February responses were: oppose the treaty, 40 percent, compared to 51 percent in September; favor the treaty, 31 percent, compared to 26 percent in September; undecided, 29 percent, compared to 23 percent in September.

Then Harris introduced a new question: "The original treaties have been changed to allow the use of U.S. military force to defend the canal in an emergency and to allow U.S. warships priority in going through the canal in an emergency. In general, do you tend to agree or disagree with these changes in the Panama Canal treaty?" There was agreement from 56 percent, disagreement from 20 percent, and the undecided were 24 percent.

We cannot tell how many who disagreed thought the provisions strengthening the U.S. right to take initiatives went too far and how many simply wanted no part of any treaty.

Of course, the question contained an error; the changes had not been passed yet, but were being debated. Yet I doubt if that affected the responses.

Then Harris introduced his version of a turnaround question: "With the new changes, do you favor or oppose the proposed treaties with Panama on the Panama Canal?"

The responses showed a turnaround, but nothing comparable to the CBS and NBC results. Instead of 60-plus percent coming around to favor the revised treaties, the responses were 38 percent in favor, 33 percent opposed, 29 percent not sure.

What can we accept as a trend? Harris in September to Harris's first question in February? The CBS turnaround to NBC's to Harris's? What about the unchanged question and virtually unchanged responses in ORC's trend? On that score, keep in mind that ORC dropped the prior questions that had been in its first poll. In that case, it still has a three-poll trend. On the other hand, what about Gallup's impeccable two-poll trend, with a diametrically different outcome?

The first of the two Panama treaties passed with only one extra vote to spare. The battle over the second treaty may be equally intense. An historic vote in the Senate may depend on the marginals in somebody's next Panama poll. Some Senators may interpret seeming changes in public opinion as responses to their first vote, and this may influence their second vote. With so many trends to choose from, much will depend on what question gets asked and how it is interpreted and reported.

IN SEARCH OF A SUPERMARKET STRATEGY:

ALBERTSON'S DRIVES ON TAMPA/ST. PETERSBURG

Douglas J. Tigert and Sylvia Ma,
University of Toronto

INTRODUCTION

An understanding of consumers' shopping behavior at the store level can contribute to product, promotion and distribution decisions of consumer goods manufacturers as well as to the complete marketing mix strategies of the retailers themselves. No one would envy the manufacturers who woke up one morning to find that all 1200 W. T. Grant discount stores, through which they had exclusive distribution rights, were closed. The food brokers who currently depend on A & P for their livelihood are having a rough time. The 1970's have been traumatic indeed for many retailers across all retail sectors. Many new store concepts are still evolving, even within a narrow definition of food retailing.

In Tampa/St. Petersburg alone, there have been three new market entries since 1974. Albertson's has opened eight new 54,000 square foot combination stores with about an equal amount of space devoted to food and non-food merchandise. Jewel Tea has opened seven or eight new Jewel-T Box stores of around 7,000 square feet, with no perishable products and few familiar brand names. Grand Union has opened its first two new stores in what is hoped to be a major re-entry into the market with fairly large traditional supermarkets. Publix is busy converting old 15-21,000 square foot stores into modern 36,000 foot stores. Kash 'N' Karry simultaneously purchased eight small, old A & P stores and opened a number of new stores all over 36,000 square feet in size.

How are the consumers reacting? Where are they shopping and why? And what is the process by which consumers identify and evaluate alternatives and make decisions? How often does that process re-occur? How much split shopping occurs? How routinized is the store choice process? How involved are consumers in food shopping? How much information do they seek out and where? Can the process be modeled with fancy equations? If we ask consumers questions, we get answers. How good are the answers? More important, how good are the questions? In a nutshell, why is it that in the same market, firms like Publix and Albertson's can generate annual sales per square foot of almost $300 when Winn-Dixie can only generate about $170 per square foot and Pantry Pride is struggling with $120-130 per square foot.

The Store Image/Store Patronage Literature

A Framework for Analysis. Figure 1 portrays a framework for analysis of consumer choice, translated to the store choice environment. Hansen [6] has suggested that one must simultaneously examine the consumer predispositional variables and what he calls the situational variables. In the retail context, the situational variables may be viewed as the market structure variables.

At the specific level, the consumer predispositional variables must eventually be translated by the consumer into some notion of what she want in a food store. Researchers have tended to operationalize those vairables as "attribute importance" variables. Consumers are queried as to how important it is that a store possess each of a number of characteristics in terms of how they choose stores.

The relationship between attribute importance and determinancy requires additional analysis. Important attributes only become salient when the alternatives in the choice process are "differentiated" with respect to the presence of the important attributes. Alpert [1] suggests a number of approaches to identifying determinant attributes including covariate analysis and "dual questioning." Both direct and indirect approaches to understanding the linkages are required.

Once the consumer has focused on her own important attributes and identified the available alternatives, she then needs a process model which combines her perceptions of the extent to which available alternatives possess the important attributes with some ordering or weighting of the relative importance of those store attributes. Granbois [5] in a major review paper on shopping behavior and preferences, concludes that little empirical research exists on competing models of the store choice process. The type of formal model one might choose depends on how one views the type of "interaction rules" that might be operating in the consumer choice process. A brief review of the competing models in store choice suggests a wide diversity of opinion as to how the consumer choice process might be operating.

Consumer Choice Models

Compensatory Models. Compensatory models, such as the multi-attribute attitude model [4], implies a weighting procedure whereby the properties possessed by an alternative on one

FIGURE 1

A FRAMEWORK FOR ANALYSIS OF THE CONSUMER

FOOD STORE CHOICE PROCESS

Predispositional Factors (Consumer Variables)	Market Structure Factors (Competitive Environment)
General Level	General Level
Values, personality, culture, life style, demographics, etc.	Number of stores, average store size, geographic dispersion (fixed variables)

NEEDS

Specific Level	Specific Level
Attribute importance (What the consumer wants in a store)	Strategic and Tactical Manipulation: price, product mix, advertising, location, store hours, service, etc.

1. Identification of alternatives

2. Perceptions (Store image)

3. Judgement procedure
    (evaluation and choice process)

4. Store(s) Choice

dimension may compensate for what it does not have on another dimension. The multi-attribute model assumes extremely complex cognitive processes on the part of the decision maker. However, if the store choice process for food is a low involvement process, then a simplistic model may do just as well.

Very little testing of the linear compensatory model has been attempted in the grocery area. One study by Wilkie and

Weinreich [12] suggests that most consumers use a relatively small number of store attributes in the store choice process and that different consumers use different numbers of attributes.

Non-Compensatory Models. Non-compensatory models are "satisficing" models in which judgements are made concerning whether or not alternatives are satisfactory on all or some selected dimensions.

i) Dominance Models. A set of alternatives that are inferior in all aspects to other alternatives are deleted from the acceptable set. This principle may not result in a decision although it may be used early in the choice process to define the choice set.

ii) Conjunctive Model. The individual uses a minimum evaluation procedure in which the multidimensional object is judged on its minimum performance on all characteristics. When using a compensatory strategy, the consumer focuses equal attention across the entire range of possible ratings for store characteristics, and allows a better than average performance on one dimension to "offset" a poorer than average performance on another dimension. In the conjunctive strategy, the consumer focuses a disproportionate amount of attention on the negative end of the evaluative continuum.

iii) Disjunctive Model. The consumer may judge a store on its best characteristics regardless of the other attributes. Now, however, a disproportionate amount of attention is focused on the positive end of the evaluative continuum.

iv) The Lexicographic Model [3]. A hierarchy of importance exists on the store attributes. Of two or more alternatives, an individual chooses that store that is rated higher on the most important attribute irrespective of the relative positions on the other store attributes. Only if two alternatives are tied (or very close to being tied) on the highest attribute does the decision maker turn to the second most important store attribute, and so on. The lexicographic model is really a constrained version of the disjunctive model.

v) Elimination by Aspects [11]. Each alternative is seen as a set of aspects. At each stage in the evaluation process, an aspect is selected on the basis of a probability proportional to the perceived importance of the aspect. All alternatives that do not include the selected aspect (at some minimum level) are eliminated. This process is continued until only one alternative is left.

Stochastic Process Model [2]. Over long periods of time, a consumer may have a fixed probability vector of store choice. That is, a consumer may shop at two or three different stores but the proportion of time (trips/dollars, etc.) she spends at each store will be fairly stable. The stochastic process model does not explain how the original choices of stores were made.

Gravity Models [7]. The probability that an individual shopper will shop at a specific supermarket is proportional to the attractiveness of that store relative to all other alternative stores and inversely proportional to the relative distance from that individual's home to the store. Attractiveness is usually measured by a proxy variable such as store size (which is in turn a proxy for assortment).

The brand choice literature shows an overwhelming dominance of research on the linear compensatory model with some recent emphasis on stochastic models. The retailing literature is extremely fractionated with little attention paid to any model. More important, the retailing literature has failed to build a linkage between stages in the store choice process. In addition, almost no attention has been paid to market structure analysis and the linkage between store choice by consumers and store performace. In short, the question of an optimal marketing strategy for supermarkets or any other type of retailer seems to have escaped notice by academics.

To go back to Figure 1 for a moment, one can pinpoint the areas where there has been a heavy emphasis on retail research but in most cases, that research has been isolated on a specific topic. Such topics include:

        i) shopper profiles
       ii) store image
      iii) attribute importance
       iv) single versus multiple store trips
        v) trading area research (gravity models)

The studies completed represent such a wide variation in scope, setting and methodology that they defy summary characterization. Not only are many studies descriptive of partial populations (students, blacks, low income households) and therefore not generalizable, they focus on partial aspects of consumer characteristics and attitude structure. One obvious finding has been the inconsistency of attribute importance rankings across studies. If the same need structure underlies the purchase of food across markets, why does such inconsistency arise? One possible answer lies in the potential impact of market structure variables on the perception of attribute importance by consumers. Different questionnaire designs and

43

measurement methodologies also contribute to the problem.

A Structured Attack on the Problem

In 1970, The Retailing and Institutional Research Programme at the University of Toronto was launched with the specific objective of answering some of the questions outlined on page two of this paper. For better or worse, questionnaires and interviewing methodology were standardized across a large number of studies in four countries in an attempt to do comparative analysis on key questions. The focus has been on store performance, attribute importance rankings and salience and particularly on the interaction between market structure variables and predispositional (consumer) variables.

Specific research topics have included:

i) Attitude change and behaviour change. The key project here involves 92 consecutive months of tracking data in two Canadian cities on attitudes towards and shopping habits at the major food chains. These data are being analyzed through bivariate econometric time series analysis to examine cause and effect directions [8].

ii) Attribute importance rankings. Some 25 studies across various retail sectors (fast food, grocery, fashion, mass merchandisers, major appliances) have utilized the same methodology to probe on attribute importance ratings in store choice. The studies cover Canada, the U.S., the Netherlands and the U.K.

iii) Cross-sectional market structure analyses. These are essentially one-time studies in major markets with the objective of diagnosing the structure of the retail environment, store performance and shopping behaviour. The Tampa/St. Petersburg study described in the following section falls into this category. A key output of these studies involves recommendations for marketing strategy by the major chains. Two similar studies in Los Angeles [9] and Amsterdam [10] were completed in 1976 and 1977.

Behind all studies, there are a number of propositions that impact on the methodologies and the operationalization of the measurement variables:

Proposition 1: Given no change in either predispositional or market structure variables, the consumer store choice process at any point in time should approximate a steady

state condition. And given no change in either predispositional or market structure variables over long periods
of time, the store choice process should approximate a
stochastic process with a stable probability vector for
many consumers across the available store offerings. A
consumer may well split her shopping across two or three
"regular" stores, but the proportion of her spending, her
trips, etc., that are apportioned across some subset of
the total store offerings should not change significantly.

Proposition 2: The original development of a store
choice/preference for any consumer can be approximated
by the disjunctive or lexicographic model. Essentially,
all stores in the evoked set are compared on the most important attribute(s) in some type of sequential process
until only one store remains. Consumers choose the store
which is the "best" on the largest number of critical
store attributes.

Proposition 3: Most consumers shop at a second store on a
fairly regular basis. Therefore, research must probe on
first and second store choice.

Proposition 4: Consumers may optimize on some store
characteristics and satisfice on others.

Proposition 5: The frequency with which any one consumer
goes through additional iterations of the store choice
process will depend on the extent to which there is a
change in her own predispositional factors or a change in
the market structure variables. If we accept the proposition that food shopping is a low involvement task with
minimal information search most of the time, then we
should not expect most consumers to go through many iterations in the short run.

Proposition 6: As a corollary of proposition 5, any chain
which hopes to gain significant market share in a trading
area will be expected to initiate a major change in the
market structure variables. Such changes might include a
significant price war, a massive new store opening programme, a large increase in advertising dollars, etc.

Proposition 7: At any point in time, there will be consumer entries into and exits from major markets. Thus,
at any point in time, some segment of the total population
will be cycling through the store choice process and en-
gaging in some form of formal and informal information
search. There is, therefore, a continuous need for supermarket chains to be providing some minimum level of infor-

45

mation to the system. During those time periods when a
great deal of competitive activity is underway, we might
expect to find a much larger portion of the total consumer
population re-evaluating the market structure. Therefore,
the frequency with which a chain should "track" its markets depends primarily on the degree of competitive churn-
ing of the market.

Proposition 8: Changes in market structure variables can
have significant impact on consumer perceptions of attribute importance. In other words, across different markets, differences in situational variables should result
in differences in consumer predispositional variables.
The direction of causation may be uni-directional.

RESEARCH FINDINGS

Attribute Importance Ratings (Tables 1-5)

1. Comparative Analysis Across Markets. Table 1 reports
on seven studies, six of which were completed by telephone and
one by in-home interview. All were major supermarket studies
(disguised sample sizes actually are as high as 3,000 respondents per market) and all utilized the open-ended technique
to ask the attribute importance questions. Only one question -
"What is the most important reason for choosing the store where
you shop most often? - is reported in this first table.

If one were unfortunate enough to stop the research after
the fourth market (North American city "D"), one would have
concluded that the world is a stable environment indeed. Approximately one-third of the respondents in these markets said
location was the most important reason and about 15 percent
said low price. These markets are all very similar in terms of
market structure. They all have 5-7 major supermarket chains
and the price spread across these chains is about 3-4 percentage points from lowest to highest priced chain.

North American City E and the two Dutch studies were completed in markets where the low price leader is 12-14 percent
lower in price than the next nearest competitor. In these
markets, price jumped into first place on the attribute importance ranking, well ahead of location in second place.

Two additional cities in North America are reported in
Table 2. In each city, two measurements about 30 days apart
suggest high stability in the short run. However, location in
city "F" received 51 percent of the total votes as the most important reason for store choice, a figure much higher than any
city reported in Table 1. In city "F", in Table 2, the compe-

TABLE 1

COMPARATIVE ATTRIBUTE IMPORTANCE DATA FOR SUPERMARKETS: SHARE OF MENTIONS GOING TO EACH RESPONSE TO THE QUESTION..."ALL THINGS CONSIDERED, WHAT IS THE SINGLE MOST IMPORTANT REASON YOU SHOP AT (_____) FOR MOST OF YOUR FOOD SHOPPING"

	CITIES						
	NORTH AMERICA					NETHERLANDS	
REASONS GIVEN*	A	B	C	D	E	TEL	IN-HOME
1. LOCATION/CONVENIENCE/ EASY TO GET TO	34%**	35%	36%	34%	27%	23%	22%
2. PRICES/LOW PRICE.........	14	18	16	13	40	33	37
3. LARGE VARIETY/WELL STOCKED/ ASSORTMENT/EVERYTHING YOU NEED...............	9	11	9	11	7	13	12
4. MEAT QUALITY/VARIETY......	11	6	8	7	5	0	0
5. OVERALL QUALITY..........	9	3	5	5	1	6	5
6. SERVICE/FRIENDLY/COURTEOUS/ FAST CHECKOUT.............	4	6	7	6	5	7	5
7. SPECIALS/SALES, COUPONS/ STAMPS/WEEKLY SPECIALS...	7	5	6	7	3	2	1
8. PLEASANT SHOPPING ENVIRONMENT.............	0	0	1	2	0	8	7

TABLE 1 (CONT'D)

| | CITIES | | | | | | |
| | NORTH AMERICA | | | | | NETHERLANDS | |
	A	B	C	D	E	TEL	IN-HOME
9. ALL OTHERS..........	12	16	12	15	12	8	11
TOTALS..............	100%	100%	100%	100%	100%	100%	100%
SAMPLE SIZE (N).......	(1000)	(1000)	(1000)	(1000)	(1000)	(1000)	(1000)

* QUESTION WAS ASKED IN OPEN-END FORM. RESPONSES WERE RECORDED VERBATIM AND LATER POST-CODED INTO THE ABOVE CATEGORIES.

** IN U.S. CITY "A", 34 PERCENT OF THE TOTAL SAMPLE SAID LOCATION/CONVENIENCE WAS THE MOST IMPOR- TANT REASON WHY THEY CHOSE THE STORE WHERE THEY DO MOST OF THEIR FOOD SPENDING.

48

TABLE 2

MEASURING THE SHORT-TERM STABILITY OF ATTRIBUTE IMPORTANCE
RATINGS IN GROCERY STORE CHOICE: A TWO-CITY COMPARISON

All Things Considered, What Is The Most Important Reason For Choosing The Store Where You Shop Most Often?	CITIES/TIME			
	City "F"		City "G"	
	T 1	T 2	T 1	T 2
1. Location/convenience/ easy to get to	51%*	52%*	44%*	44%*
2. Lowest prices/prices/ good prices, etc. . .	15	13	12	15
3. Good service/friendly/ courteous/fast checkout	6	6	8	7
4. Large variety/well stocked/good variety/ everything I need, etc.	6	4	7	7
5. Cleanliness/clean/ neat stores, etc.. . .	5	5	3	6
6. Nice stores/pleasant shopping environment .	3	5	3	4
7. Overall quality of merchandise.	3	3	7	5
8. Good meat quality/ meat variety	4	4	6	5
9. Good produce/fresh produce.	2	4	2	3
10. Weekly specials/special sales/coupons.	2	2	3	2
11. All others	3	2	5	2
TOTALS.	100%	100%	100%	100%
(Sample size).	(1000)	(1000)	(1000)	(1000)

* Read: In city "F," 1,000 respondents were asked for the most

49

important reason they chose the store where they shopped most often. Fifty-one percent of those respondents said location/convenience/easy to get to was the most important reason. That figure rose to 52 percent for a second independent matched sample 30 days later. The question was asked in an open-ended manner, by telephone.

---

titive environment is very constrained. Three chains capture 85 percent of the total market and the price spread across those three chains is less than two percentage points. Consumers clearly perceive little motivation to go beyond the most convenient store.

Table 3 reports on the Tampa/St. Petersburg market. Here, the data on "most important reason" reverts back to a one-third share of mentions for location, 20 percent for low price and 10 percent for assortment, figures that are quite close to North American cities "A" through "D". In the Tampa/St. Petersburg market (TSP), there are six major competitors and the price spread is 4.6 percentage points.

Table 4 shows the fallacy of imputing any interpretation to the rankings beyond the first and second most important reason for store choice, from questions which ask respondents for their first and second most important reasons.

In Table 3, assortment/selection received the third highest share of mentions as the "first" or "second" most important reasons for choosing the store where respondents shop most often. However, the respondents who mentioned location or price as the first or second most important reason did not mention a third choice. We did not ask the third choice question.

In Table 4, respondents were asked how they would choose from a subset of stores that were all equal on location and price. The first three reasons given by respondents are reported in Table 4. Thus, while assortment/selection receives 10 percent of the votes for most important reason, it also only receives 12 percent of the votes on (third) most important after controlling for price and location. One might conclude that about 25 percent of consumers feel that assortment is first or second most important in choosing their preferred store (from Table 3) but that for the remainder of the market, assortment/selection rates no better than fifth or sixth most important.

Table 5 examines the shoppers of each of the major chains for significant differences in how they view attribute impor-

50

TABLE 3

TAMPA/ST. PETERSBURG

MOST IMPORTANT REASONS FOR SHOPPING WHERE SHOP MOST OFTEN: ATTRIBUTE IMPORTANCE

	Most Important	Second Most Important	Total 1st & 2nd Mentions	Average
LOCATION/ CONVENIENCE.	31%*	15%	46%	23%
LOW PRICES/PRICES. .	20	10	30	15
ASSORTMENT/SELECTION/ VARIETY.	10	15	25	13
SERVICE/FRIENDLY, COURTEOUS/FAST CHECKOUT	8	12	20	10
CLEANLINESS.	8	10	18	9
MEAT QUALITY/VARIETY	7	7	14	7
OVERALL QUALITY. . .	3	5	8	4
WEEKLY SPECIALS/ COUPONS.	3	3	6	3
PRODUCE QUALITY/ VARIETY.	3	5	8	4
NICE STORE/SHOPPING ENVIRONMENT.	2	3	5	2
OTHERS	5	10	15	7
NONE/NO OTHER. . . .	0	5	5	3
TOTALS . . .	100%	100%	100%	100%

*READ: 31 percent of respondents said location/convenience was
    the most important reason why they chose the store where
    they shop most often.

TABLE 4

TAMPA/ST. PETERSBURG

CONTROLLING FOR PRICE AND LOCATION,
WHAT ARE THE MOST IMPORTANT STORE CHOICE ATTRIBUTES

	1st Mention	2nd Mention	3rd Mention	Totals
CLEANLINESS.	28%*	17%	9%	54%
SERVICE/FRIENDLY/ COURTEOUS/FAST CHECKOUT	25	23	11	59
ASSORTMENT VARIETY . .	12	10	10	32
MEAT QAULITY/VARIETY .	10	8	5	23
NICE STORE/SHOPPING ENVIRONMENT.	4	4	4	12
PRODUCE QUALITY/VARIETY	4	8	6	18
OVERALL QUALITY . . .	4	4	2	10
WEEKLY SPECIALS/COUPONS	4	2	2	8
ALL OTHERS	4	4	3	11
NONE/NO OTHERS	5	20	48	73
TOTALS	100%	100%	100%	300%

* READ: When asked how they would choose a store where they would shop most often, from among a set of stores they were equal on location and price, 28 percent of the total sample said cleanliness was the first factor they would consider.

52

TABLE 5

TAMPA/ST. PETERSBURG: SHARE OF MENTIONS GOING TO EACH REASON ON
..."MOST IMPORTANCE REASON YOU SHOP WHERE YOU SHOP MOST OFTEN"...

Reasons Given	Total Sample	Store Shop Most Often					
		Albertsons	Kash 'N' Karry	Pantry Pride	Publix	Winn-Dixie	U-Save
1. LOCATION/CONVENIENCE.	31%	4%**	30%	(37%)	30%	(42%)	30%
2. LOW PRICES.	20	11	(32)	(32)	4	16	(44)
3. ASSORTMENT/SELECTION.	10	(30)	12	11	12	7	4
4. SERVICE	8	(17)	9	3	9	5	10
5. CLEANLINESS	8	8	2	2	(17)	2	3
6. MEAT QUALITY/VARIETY.	7	6	4	2	6	(13)	3
7. OVERALL QUALITY	3	4	2	0	5	1	1
8. WEEKLY SPECIALS/COUPONS . . .	3	0	1	0	2	(8)	2
9. PRODUCE QUALITY/VARIETY . . .	3	4	1	5	5	0	0
10. SHOPPING ENVIRONMENT.	2	2	1	0	3	3	0

53

TABLE 5 (CONT'D.)

		Store Shop Most Often					
Reasons Given	Total Sample	Albertsons	Kash 'N' Karry	Pantry Pride	Publix	Winn-Dixie	U-Save
11. OTHERS	5	14	6	8	7	3	3
	100%	100%	100%	100%	100%	100%	100%
SAMPLE SIZE	(990)	(53)	(211)	(38)	(335)	(196)	(70)

*READ: Only 4 percent of those who shop most often at Albertson's said location/convenience was the most important reason for choosing that store.

54

tance. The magnitude of differences is staggering. For Winn-
Dixie, 42 percent of the shoppers said location was the most
important store choice variable with price and meat in relatively weak second and third place positions. Winn-Dixie has
low sales per square foot and appears to be heavily dependent
on its own trading area. That conclusion is confirmed in a
later table. For U-Save, low price is clearly the driving
force that its shoppers say they are looking for. U-Save is,
in fact, one of the two low price leaders in the market, along
with Kash 'N' Karry (see Table 9). Albertson's, the super com-
bo store in the market, appears to attract customers who are
looking primarily for assortment and also service. Albertson's
has by far the largest assortment in the market. All eight
stores are 54,000 square feet with the next largest average
store size falling to 30,000 for Kash 'N' Karry.

Clearly, Tables 1-4 lead to several conclusions. Attribute importance scores differ widely across markets depending
on the differentiation in market structure variables. Attribute importance scores also differ markedly across the shoppers
of different chains in the same market, suggesting differential
appeals of the chains. The next obvious question is, what appeal is the most successful. In other words, what store characteristics draw a disproportionately high share of shoppers to
a chain....more than it deserves on the basis of location
alone? And what is the role of location itself?

Retail Image and Store Performance: Tampa/St. Petersburg

Can Consumers Answer Simple Questions? Following the
model that consumers choose stores on the basis of which one(s)
is (are) best on the largest number of critical store characteristics, the measurement methodology chosen to probe on store
image was the "associative" technique. For each of a set of 24
store characteristics, respondents were asked which one chain
was the "best" on that dimension. Table 6 reports on how consumers answered those questions. In spite of the fact that
they were asked to single out one specific chain, some consumers mentioned more than one chain on some questions. Nine percent of the respondents said two or more chains were the best
on cleanliness (equally as good). In addition, on some dimensions, as many as 20 percent of respondents said they didn't
know who was best. It is interesting to speculate what type of
data would be generated if all respondents were asked to scale
all stores on all dimensions. As will be shown later, on almost all dimensions, the store mentioned as being the best
tended to be the store where respondents either shopped most
often or second most often. Most consumers have detailed familiarity with only two or three stores.

TABLE 6

TAMPA/ST. PETERSBURG: PERCENTAGE OF MENTIONS GOING TO
"DON'T KNOW" OR TO "MULTIPLE MENTIONS" FOR EACH STORE
CHARACTERISTIC

WHICH STORE IS (OR HAS).	Don't Know	Multiple Mention
1. The easiest one to get to from home. .	0%*	3%*
2. Store shopped, last major food trip. .	0	2
3. Store shopped most often	0	1
4. Best overall assortment/variety of food products.	2	6
5. The cleanest stores.	2	9
6. The best quality fresh produce	2	4
7. The most pleasant shopping environment	2	4
8. Store shopped second most often. . . .	3	2
9. Best at being in-stock with items you need	3	6
10. Best variety/selection of fresh meat .	3	4
11. Best overall customer service.	4	6
12. Best quality fresh meat.	4	5
13. Fastest checkout counters.	5	6
14. Most courteous, friendly staff	5	8
15. Best specialty baked goods dept. . . .	6	2
16. Best delicatessen department	6	1
17. Best overall advertising	7	8
18. Best assortment of non-food merchandise.	8	3
19. Lowest prices.	8	4

TABLE 6 (CONT'D.)

WHICH STORE IS (OR HAS).	Don't Know	Multiple Mention
20. Highest prices	13	3
21. Best quality private label brands. . .	17	3
22. Another store just as easy to get to or almost as easy to get to from home.	20	8

*Read: When 1,000 respondents were asked which store was the easiest one to get to from their home, no one said "I don't know" but 30 respondents mentioned more than one chain.

One might also hypothesize that dimensions which generate a large percentage of "don't know" or multiple mention responses are less salient in the store choice process, at least for primary shopping.

Overall Ratings On The Chains From The Total Sample. Table 7 reports on the total share of mentions going to each chain on each characteristic, from the total sample. The table is inserted merely to indicate that most chains have a high variance across the store characteristics in terms of their share of mentions. For example, only 9 percent of respondents said Publix had the lowest prices, but 60 percent of all respondents said Publix had the cleanest stores. Albertson's share of mentions ranges between five percent (location) and 40 percent (assortment).

Consumer Perceptions and External Validity. For the major chains, the overall share of mentions can be checked against external market data. Table 8 looks at the relationship between perceived and actual market coverage. Winn-Dixie, for example, has 26 percent of the total square feet of store space in the market and 26 percent of respondents said Winn-Dixie was the closest store to their home. Thus the consumer perception data is a perfect match for an external measurement. However, not all chains come out that close. Publix has 24 percent of the square feet and 28 percent of the perceived coverage. One might hypothesize that Publix has above average locations or that with an above average performance (which it has) Publix tends to get mentioned as being the most convenient store by people who are really equally close to Publix and another store. However, in general, what Table 8 demonstrates is that perceived coverage is very close to share of square feet and

TABLE 7

TAMPA/ST. PETERSBURG: SHARE OF MENTIONS GOING TO EACH CHAIN ON EACH STORE CHARACTERISTIC

	(1) Market Coverage: Store Easiest To Get To From Home	(2) Last Major Food Shopping Trip	(3) Ratio: Last Shopped/Market Coverage (2÷1)	(4) Shopped Most Often	(5) Ratio: Shop Most Often/Coverage (4÷1)	(6) Shop Second Most Often
PUBLIX.............	27%*	32%	1.18/1	34%	1.26/1	25%
KASH 'N' KARRY.....	22	20	.91/1	21	.95/1	16
WINN-DIXIE.........	25	19	.76/1	20	.80/1	25
U-SAVE.............	9	8	.89/1	7	.78/1	7
ALBERTSON'S........	5	8	1.60/1	5	1.00/1	10
PANTRY PRIDE.......	6	4	.67/1	4	.67/1	6
FOOD WORLD.........	1	2	2.00/1	2	2.00/1	2
BIG STAR...........	1	1	1.00/1	1	1.00/1	2
GRAND UNION........	1	1	1.00/1	1	1.00/1	1
JEWEL-T............	0	0	-	0	-	1
ALL OTHERS.........	3	5	1.67/1	5	1.67/1	5
TOTALS....	100%	100%		100%		100%

*READ: 27 percent of all respondents said PUBLIX was the easiest store to get to from home.

TABLE 7 (CONT'D.)

Store Mentioned	(7) Total Primary Plus Secondary Shoppers (6 + 4)	(8) Lowest Prices	(9) Highest Prices	(10) Ratio: Lowest/ Highest Prices (8 + 9)	(11) Best Overall Assortment/ Variety of Food Products	(12) Best Overall Assortment of Non-Food Merchandise
PUBLIX.........	59%	9%	66%	.14/1	49%	19%
KASH 'N' KARRY......	37	33	3	11.00/1	16	17
WINN–DIXIE........	45	18	13	1.38/1	9	13
U–SAVE........	14	15	1	15.00/1	4	5
ALBERTSON'S........	15	7	8	.88/1	(16)	(40)
PANTRY PRIDE........	10	7	4	1.75/1	2	3
FOOD WORLD.........	4	3	0	3.00/0	1	1
BIG STAR.........	3	2	1	2.00/1	1	0
GRAND UNION.........	1	2	0	2.00/0	0	0
JEWEL–T.........	1	2	0	2.00/0	0	0
ALL OTHERS.........	10	2	4	0.50/1	2	2
TOTALS....	200%	100%	100%		100%	100%

TABLE 7 (CONT'D.)

Store Mentioned	(13) Best at Being In-stock	(14) Cleanest Stores	(15) Best Overall Customer Service	(16) Fastest Checkout Counters	(17) Most Friendly Courteous Staff	(18) Best Quality Fresh Meat	(19) Best Variety/ Selection Fresh Meat
PUBLIX.............	45%	60%	49%	38%	40%	43%	44%
KASH 'N' KARRY......	19	14	18	20	21	13	13
WINN-DIXIE..........	13	9	13	17	16	(26)	22
U-SAVE.............	6	3	5	5	7	5	4
ALBERTSON'S.........	10	10	9	12	8	4	9
PANTRY PRIDE.........	3	2	3	4	4	2	3
FOOD WORLD..........	1	1	1	1	1	1	1
BIG STAR...........	0	0	1	1	1	1	1
GRAND UNION.........	0	0	0	0	0	0	1
JEWEL-T............	0	0	0	0	0	0	0
ALL OTHERS.........	3	0	1	2	2	5	2
TOTALS...	100%	100%	100%	100%	100%	100%	100%

TABLE 7 (CONT'D.)

Store Mentioned	(20) Best Quality Produce	(21) Most Pleasant Shopping Environment	(22) Best Overall Advertising	(23) Best Weekly Specials	(24) Best Quality Private Label Brands	(25) Best Specialty Baked Goods
PUBLIX...........	55%	51%	50%	37%	32%	57%
KASH 'N' KARRY......	11	14	11	12	13	5
WINN-DIXIE..........	7	12	22	(33)	(29)	13
U-SAVE..............	4	4	2	4	7	2
ALBERTSON'S.........	11	12	10	5	5	(18)
PANTRY PRIDE........	5	2	1	2	8	1
FOOD WORLD..........	2	2	1	3	1	1
BIG STAR............	0	0	0	1	0	0
GRAND UNION.........	0	0	1	1	1	0
JEWEL-T.............	0	0	0	0	1	0
ALL OTHERS..........	5	3	2	2	3	3
TOTALS...	100%	100%	100%	100%	100%	100%

TABLE 7 (CONT'D.)

	(26) Best Delicatessen Department
PUBLIX............	63%
KASH 'N' KARRY......	2
WINN-DIXIE..........	16
U-SAVE............	1
ALBERTSON'S........	11
PANTRY PRIDE........	2
FOOD WORLD.........	2
BIG STAR..........	0
GRAND UNION........	0
JEWEL-T...........	0
ALL OTHERS........	3
TOTALS....	100%

TABLE 8

TAMPA/ST. PETERSBURG: RELATIONSHIP BETWEEN PERCEIVED
MARKET COVERAGE AND ACTUAL MARKET COVERAGE

CHAINS	SHARE OF PERCEIVED COVERAGE	SHARE OF SQUARE FEET (GLA)	SHARE OF STORES	SHARE OF SHOPPERS
1. PUBLIX...........	28%*	24%*	23%*	34%*
2. WINN-DIXIE.......	26	26	29	20
3. KASH 'N' KARRY...	23	20	21	21
4. PANTRY PRIDE.....	6	10	10	4
5. U-SAVE...........	9	7	6	9
6. ALBERTSON'S......	5	8**	3**	9
7. BIG STAR.........	1	2	3	1
8. GRAND UNION......	1	1	1	1
9. FOOD WORLD.......	1	1	1	2
10. JEWEL-T BOX STORES	0	1	3	0
	100%	100%	100%	100%

*Read: Twenty-eight percent of the Tampa/St. Petersburg sample
said Publix was the easiest store to get to from their
home. Publix has 24 percent of the actual square feet
of gross leasable area (GLA) occupied by the store set
above and 23 percent of the total stores in the market.
However, Publix has 34 percent of the shoppers (store
last shopped). Above figures eliminate all other
stores and re-compute to 100 percent.

** Albertson's had 8 stores open at the time of the survey.
However, two of them had only been open a month and two
others for about four months. The Albertson's figures are
based on an average of 6 stores. Albertson's stores are the
only ones open 24 hours a day, 7 days a week.

that some firms have a much higher market share than they do market coverage. Those chains tend to be the high performers.

One can also use the shoppers/coverage ratios to predict sales per square foot figures. The two chains with the best shoppers/coverage ratios, combining both <u>shop most often</u> and <u>shop second most often</u> (among major chains) are Publix and Albertson's. These chains do about $270-280 a year in sales per square foot on gross leasable area. The chain with the worst shoppers/coverage ratio, Pantry Pride, does only about $130 per square foot per year.

Finally, Tables 9 and 10 examine the relationship between actual and perceived prices. A price basket of 120 items, including fresh meat and produce and non-food merchandise was used to measure actual prices. The price ratio, a measure of share of mentions on "lowest prices"/share of mentions on "highest prices" has proven to be a driving force in a causal direction in changing share of shoppers in our econometric analysis of time series tracking data [8]. Table 10 indicates some, but not complete agreement between actual and perceived price positions in the TSP market. Two chains are out of order. Albertson's and Publix's price ratios should be higher. However, Albertson's is a recent entry into the market and Publix has only recently become more price competitive. Its prices were very close to those of Winn-Dixie only a short time ago. In general, the two price leaders, Kash 'N' Karry and U-Save have the two best price ratios on the price image data.

<u>Analyzing the Determinants of Patronage and Performance</u>. Table 11 examines the image of each chain among its own customers. The reader may wish to go back and examine the attribute importance data to see if those dimensions on which each chain receives a high score from its own shoppers are the same dimensions which that store's shoppers said were the most important dimensions on which they chose their preferred store.

What is more interesting, however, is the high variance across chains in terms of the strength of the overall image among its own customers across the store dimensions. Publix, for example, has an average score of 74 percent, treating each store characteristically equally (assuming no weights from the attribute importance data). Figure 2 shows that Publix, with the highest average score in Table 11 has the highest sales per square foot in the market. Pantry Pride and U-Save, with low average scores in Table 11, have low sales per square foot. The relationship is not perfect. Figure 2 also examines the data for chains in Los Angeles as well as TSP. Four L.A. chains -- Alpha Beta, Albertson's, Lucky and Gemco -- all have average scores among their own shoppers of about 55 percent and

64

TABLE 9

TAMPA/ST. PETERSBURG PRICE BASKET, FEB., 1978*

	Meat	Produce	Groceries	General Merchandise	Totals	Percent Above Market Leader
K.K..................	$ 39.34	$ 13.53	$ 97.38	$ 21.39	$ 171.64	–
U-SAVE..............	39.80	13.66	96.92	21.81	172.19	0.3%
FOOD WORLD..........	39.01	14.24	97.90	22.08	173.03	0.8%
ALBERTSON'S.........	40.81	14.08	98.98	21.55	175.42	2.2%
WEBB'S CITY.........	39.10	14.44	101.48	22.15	177.17	3.2%
PUBLIX.............	39.67	13.86	101.58	22.64	177.75	3.6%
BIG STAR............	40.81	13.31	102.38	22.64	179.14	4.4%
P. PRIDE...........	40.23	14.62	101.75	22.76	179.36	4.5%
WINN-DIXIE..........	41.15	14.10	101.67	22.15	179.57	4.6%

The price basket contains 120 items, including perishables and non-food merchandise. All branded goods are national brands. To the extent that a chain has an above average share of sales in private label (store's own) brands, the price basket may over or under represent its true price position.

TABLE 10

TAMPA/ST. PETERSBURG: RELATIONSHIP BETWEEN ACTUAL AND
PERCEIVED MARKET PRICES

CHAIN COVERED	TOTAL PRICE BASKET	PERCENT ABOVE MARKET LEADER	RATIO: SHARE OF MENTIONS LOWEST PRICES/ HIGHEST PRICES
KASH 'N' KARRY.......	$171.64	- - -	11.0/1
U-SAVE..............	172.19	0.3%*	15.0/1*
FOOD WORLD..........	173.03	0.8	3.0/0
ALBERTSON'S.........	175.42	2.2	0.9/1
PUBLIX..............	177.75	3.6	0.1/1**
BIG STAR............	179.14	4.4	2.0/1
PANTRY PRIDE........	179.36	4.5	1.7/1
WINN-DIXIE..........	179.57	4.6	1.4/1

*Read: U-Save's prices are less than 1 percent (0.3%) higher than those of Kash 'N' Karry, the market price leader. When respondents were asked who had the lowest and highest prices in the market, 15 percent said U-Save had the lowest prices and 1 percent said U-Save had the highest prices.

** Publix received 9 percent on "lowest prices," 66 percent on "highest prices," for a ratio of 0.1/1. Publix has historically been the highest priced chain in the market, a factor which has given it such a dominant position on "highest prices" mentions.

TABLE 11

SUMMARY: SHARE OF MENTIONS GOING TO EACH CHAIN AMONG THOSE
WHO SHOP MOST OFTEN AT THAT SAME CHAIN

Store Characteristics	Store Shopped Most Often					
	Albertson's	Kash 'N' Karry	Pantry Pride	Publix	Winn-Dixie	U-Save
1. Easiest to get to from home..........	(54%*)	70%	74%	68%	76%	80%
2. 2nd store just as easy to get to from home.........	(6)	13	11	13	12	11
3. Lowest prices.............	46*	(77)	65	25	51	(85)
4. Best overall assortment of food products.............	(87)	51	34	(82)	33	41
5. Best overall assortment of non-food products.........	(98)	47	21	35	31	28
6. Best at being in-stock..........	71	65	49	(87)	50	63
7. Cleanest stores.............	81	46	40	(91)	31	27
8. Best overall customer service......	71	65	56	(90)	52	59
9. Fastest checkout counters.........	(82)	64	43	73	54	51

TABLE 11 (CONT'D.)

| | | Store Shopped Most Often | | | | |
Store Characteristics	Albertson's	Kash 'N' Karry	Pantry Pride	Publix	Winn-Dixie	U-Save
10. Most friendly, courteous staff.....	70%	75%	55%	(87%)	63%	70%
11. Best quality fresh meat..........	37	44	33	(70)	58	44
12. Best variety selection of fresh meat........	56	42	30	(70)	52	32
13. Best quality produce...........	64	33	42	(78)	20	33
14. Most pleasant shopping environment.	(88)	54	42	(88)	44	44
15. Best overall advertising........	45	34	19	(77)	54	15
16. Best weekly specials...........	48	39	41	(71)	70	25
17. Best quality private label brands..	46	47	(82)	66	74	61
18. Best specialty baked goods dept....	71	16	16	(82)	27	13
19. Best delicatessen dept............	48	5	22	(83)	39	10
Total Score..............	(1109)	(804)	(690)	(1255)	(803)	(701)

68

TABLE 11 (CONT'D.)

Store Characteristics	Store Shopped Most Often					
	Albertson's	Kash 'N' Karry	Pantry Pride	Publix	Winn-Dixie	U-Save
Average, Items (3-19).............	(65%)	(47%)	(41%)	(74%)	(47%)	(41%)
Average, weighted by attribute importance scores for each chain's shoppers for Q3, 4, 7 8, 9, 10, 11, 12, 13, 14, 16......	(73%)	(63%)	(55%)	(79%)	(52%)	(72%)

*READ: Among those who shop most often at ALBERTSON'S, 54% also said Albertson's was easiest to get to, 46% said Albertson's had the lowest prices, etc.

69

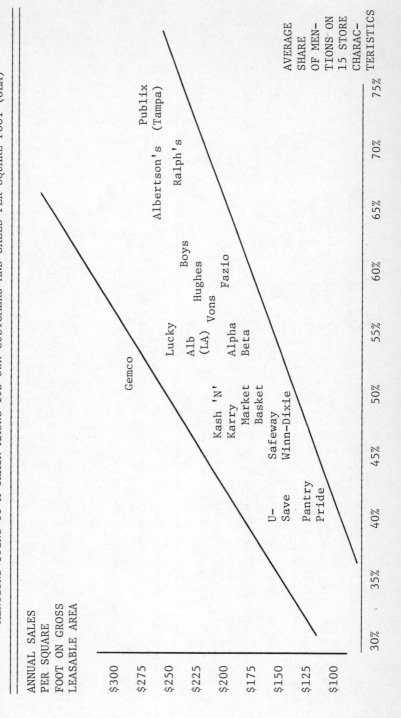

FIGURE 2

LOS ANGELES AND TAMPA/ST. PETERSBURG: RELATIONSHIP BETWEEN AVERAGE SHARE OF
MENTIONS GOING TO A CHAIN AMONG ITS OWN CUSTOMERS AND SALES PER SQUARE FOOT (GLA)

70

have a range on performance between $180 per square foot and
$280 per square foot. Gemco in L.A. does it all on low price
leadership. Clearly low price ranks very high on importance as
a store choice variable for Gemco shoppers. What Figure 2 does
show is that a naive model can provide a lot of diagnostic
data. The TSP market has only two high performers in Publix
and Albertson's. After that, it's a long way down to the next
best chain. L.A. on the other hand, is a highly competitive
market with 9 chains all better than the third best chain in
TSP. Albertson's clearly chose well in entering the TSP market where the competition was woefully weak. Many chains in
that market are living on borrowed time. Albertson's does
$275/sq. ft. in TSP and only about $210-220/sq. ft. in Los Angeles.

Secondary Shopper Analysis. When TSP respondents were
asked if there was another store where they shopped second most
often, all but five percent indicated a second store. While
they were not asked how often they shopped there relative to
their preferred store, focussed group research has, in other
markets, substantiated the finding that secondary stores are
heavily patronized by more than half of all grocery shoppers.
Table 12 examines the shopper ratings of the various chains for
secondary shopping. Since many consumers mention the store
where they shop most often when they are asked who is the best
on something, the scores in Table 12 are much lower than the
scores in Table 11. However, Publix and Albertson's again
stand out well ahead of the other chain on average scores. In
fact, across 25 markets, Publix has the highest secondary shopper profile yet measured. Their average score of 46 percent
compares to only 35 percent for Ralph's, the best chain in Los
Angeles. Albertson's in TSP, with a 34 percent average score,
rates about as well as Ralph's in L.A. Again, the wide dis-
parity between Publix and Albertson's at the top in TSP, and
the rest of the chains indicates a weak competitive market.

Weighting of the mentions for each chain by the attribute
importance scores does not improve the prediction of sales per
square foot. In fact, the weightings worsen the prediction.
Yet, the strongest dimensions for each chain tend to be the
ones which its own customers rate highest on attribute importance. The problem lies in the weighting procedure. Work is
in progress to fine-tune the analysis.

Can Store Loyalty Overcome Location? In an attempt to
ascertain the degree of loyalty consumers exhibited toward
their own chain, respondents were asked what they would do if
the one specific store where they shopped were to close down.
Would customers move to another outlet of the same chain or
would they switch to another outlet of a different chain that

71

TABLE 12

TAMPA/ST. PETERSBURG, 1978: SHARE OF MENTIONS GOING TO
EACH CHAIN AMONG THOSE WHO SHOP SECOND MOST OFTEN AT THAT CHAIN

Store Characteristics	Store Shopped Second Most Often					
	Albertson's	Kash 'N' Karry	Pantry Pride	Publix	Winn-Dixie	U-Save
1. Easiest to get to from home........	17%*	24%*	31%	17%	37%	32%
2. Equally as easy to get to from home	$\frac{23}{40}$	$\frac{41}{65}$	$\frac{31}{62}$	$\frac{30}{47}$	$\frac{40}{67}$	$\frac{29}{61}$
3. Lowest overall prices.............	19*	50	28	7	20	52
4. Best quality fresh meat...........	13	17	5	41	32	10
5. Best assortment/variety fresh meat.	32	16	9	45	27	12
6. Best overall customer service......	32	19	4	47	10	12
7. Fastest checkout counters.........	41	29	18	35	18	18
8. Most friendly, courteous staff.....	21	24	19	32	11	14
9. Best quality produce.............	45	20	29	69	11	20
10. Best weekly "specials"..............	9	17	2	35	45	12

TABLE 12 (CONT'D.)

			Store Shopped Second Most Often			
Store Characteristics	Albertson's	Kash 'N' Karry	Pantry Pride	Publix	Winn-Dixie	U-Save
11. Best quality private label brands...	20	17	24	30	31	20
12. Best overall assortment/variety of food products...	51	22	6	52	6	12
13. Largest assortment of non-food merchandise...	89	29	6	21	16	23
14. Best overall advertising...	24	8	8	59	28	7
15. Cleanest stores...	33	17	7	59	7	11
16. Best at being in-stock...	31	21	6	46	10	19
17. Best specialty baked goods...	52	7	2	70	18	9
18. Best delicatessen department...	38	3	7	76	16	7
19. Most pleasant shopping environment.	36	11	10	54	10	8
A. Total score...	586	327	191	778	316	266
B. Average Items (3-19)...	(34%)	(19%)	(11%)	(46%)	(19%)	(16%)

TABLE 12 (CONT'D.)

| Store Characteristics | Store Shopped Second Most Often | | | | | |
	Albertson's	Kash 'N' Karry	Pantry Pride	Publix	Winn-Dixie	U-Save
C. # Scores Over 30%............	11	1	0	15	3	1

*READ: Among those who shop second most often at Albertson's, 17 percent said Albertson's was easiest to get to from home, 19 percent said Albertson's had the lowest prices, etc.

0 = Best scores on that store characteristic

74

was close to their home? The data in Table 13 indicate that over half the customers of all chains would switch to a different chain. Even the comparative data in the circled diagonal percentages is misleading. Albertson's would appear to have the lowest store loyalty position. However, Albertson's has only 8 stores in the market with large distances between stores. Publix and Winn-Dixie have over 40 stores each. Thus, while one might be willing to concede that Publix has a higher loyalty factor than Winn-Dixie, one cannot do comparative analysis across stores with high variance in the number of stores.

TABLE 13

TAMPA/ST. PETERSBURG STORE LOYALTY ANALYSIS: STORE SHOPPED MOST OFTEN VERSUS STORE CHOICE IF CURRENT STORE WERE TO CLOSE DOWN

IF THE ONE SPECIFIC STORE WHERE YOU SHOP MOST OFTEN WERE TO CLOSE DOWN, WHERE WOULD YOU SHOP MOST OFTEN	STORE SHOPPED MOST OFTEN NOW					
	Albertson's	Kash 'N' Karry	Pantry Pride	Publix	Winn-Dixie	U-Save
ALBERTSON'S....	26%*	5%	9%	11%	9%	6%
KASH 'N' KARRY.	8	38	9	14	20	25
PANTRY PRIDE...	6	4	35	2	5	3
PUBLIX.........	30	21	18	46	20	15
WINN-DIXIE.....	17	16	23	21	37	13
U-SAVE.........	13	8	3	2	5	31
ALL OTHERS.....	0	8	3	4	4	7
TOTALS.....	100%	100%	100%	100%	100%	100%
(Sample Size)..	(53)	(202)	(34)	(319)	(189)	(67)

*READ: When those who said they currently shop Albertson's most often were asked where they would shop most often if the one specific Albertson's were to close down, 26 percent said they would seek out another Albertson's. The table measures the extent to which consumers would stay with their current chain and the extent to which there is another store in the same chain that is reasonably accessible. Albertson's, with only 8 widely scattered stores in the market appears to have the worst loyalty rating when in fact the real problem is lack of market coverage.

Analyzing the Leverage Factors. Tables 14 and 15 look at the store image data in a different way for two chains: Publix and Winn-Dixie. For each store characteristic, all respondents who say a particular store is best are then examined in terms of their shopping habits at that same chain. A number of important conclusions can be drawn from that analysis:

i) upwards of 100 percent of respondents who say a particular chain is best on something also shop that chain either most often or at least second most often.

ii) the degree, however, to which respondents shop the chain most often versus second most often varies greatly depending on which store characteristic we are examining.

iii) the degree to which being best on something generates primary shoppers for a chain rather than secondary shoppers is extremely critical because primary shoppers spend a great deal more at a chain than do secondary shoppers.

iv) the critical leverage variables for Publix are location (build more stores), price (the chain needs to become more price competitive), and service. The chain would attract almost 100 percent of consumers in new trading areas to its store, and they would primarily be shopping Publix most often.

v) for Winn-Dixie, building more stores would not be nearly as successful because Winn-Dixie has the wrong type of store. Winn-Dixie's leverage variables are assortment (build bigger stores or increase store size or improve current assortment), service and being in-stock (another problem with Winn-Dixie's assortment). Clearly, Winn-Dixie's stores are too small, but for those respondents who feel WD's assortments are adequate, a high percentage shop there most often. Winn-Dixie's challenge is to convince more consumers that they have adequate assortments. They can only push that button by increasing store size. They currently have the smallest average store size in the market.

vi) clearly the only stores that respondents can talk about in terms of who is best, are the stores they patronize a good deal of the time. It is highly probably that consumers do the bulk of their shopping at only two chains. That concentration of shopping

TABLE 14

TAMPA/ST. PETERSBURG: ANALYZING THE LEVERAGE FACTORS FOR WINN-DIXIE.
AMONG THOSE WHO SAY YOU ARE THE BEST ON SOMETHING, WHAT PERCENTAGE SHOP
YOU EITHER MOST OFTEN OR SECOND MOST OFTEN?

AMONG THOSE WHO SAY WINN-DIXIE...........	What Percent Shop Winn-Dixie		Ratio: Shop Most Often/ Shop Second Most Often	Rank
	Most Often	Second Most Often		
1. Has the most courteous, friendly staff (16% of sample)...............	76%	18%	4.22/1	1
2. Has the largest overall assortment/ variety of food products (9% of sample)..	71	17	4.17/1	2
3. Has the best overall customer service (13% of sample)...............	75	20	3.75/1	3
4. Is the best at being in-stock with items they need (13% of sample)...........	77	21	3.66/1	4
5. Has the most pleasant shopping environ- ment (12% of sample)...............	73	22	3.31/1	5
6. Has the cleanest stores (9% of sample)....	69	22	3.13/1	6
7. Has the fastest checkout counters (17% of sample)...............	61	27	2.25/1	7

77

TABLE 14 (CONT'D.)

AMONG THOSE WHO SAY WINN-DIXIE.........	What Percent Shop Winn-Dixie		Ratio: Shop Most Often/ Shop Second Most Often	Rank
	Most Often	Second Most Often		
8. Is the easiest to get to from home (25% of sample).................	60%	27	2.22/1	8
9. Has the best quality private label brands (29% of sample).............	54	25	2.16/1	9
10. Has the lowest prices (18% of sample)..	58	27	2.14/1	10
11. Has the best delicatessen department (16% of sample).................	48	26	1.84/1	11
12. Has the best overall assortment of non-food merchandise (13% of sample)......	48	30	1.60/1	12
13. Has the best variety/assortment of meat (22% of sample)................	46	30	1.53/1	13
14. Has the best quality meat (26% of sample)................	45	30	1.50/1	14
15. Has the best overall advertising (23% of sample)................	46	32	1.43/1	15
16. Has the best quality produce (7% of sample).................	53	38	1.39/1	16

TABLE 14 (CONT'D.)

AMONG THOSE WHO SAY WINN-DIXIE.........	What Percent Shop Winn-Dixie		Ratio: Shop Most Often/ Shop Second Most Often	
	Most Often	Second Most Often		Rank
17. Has the best weekly "specials" (33% of sample)................	42%	34%	1.23/1	17
18. Has the best specialty baked goods department (13% of sample).............	40	33	1.21/1	18
19. Has the highest prices (13% of sample)	17	22	0.77/1	19

*READ: In the total sample of 1,000 respondents, 16 percent said Winn-Dixie has the most courteous, friendly staff. Of that group, 76 percent also shop Winn-Dixie most often and a further 18 percent shop Winn-Dixie second most often.

79

TABLE 15

TAMPA/ST. PETERSBURG: ANALYZING THE LEVERAGE FACTORS FOR PUBLIX.
AMONG THOSE WHO SAY YOU ARE THE BEST ON SOMETHING, WHAT PERCENTAGE
SHOP YOU EITHER MOST OFTEN OR SECOND MOST OFTEN

AMONG THOSE WHO SAY PUBLIX......	What Percent Shop Publix		Ratio: Shop Most Often/ Shop Second Most Often	Rank
	Most Often	Second Most Often		
1. Is easiest to get to from home (27% of total sample)............	83%	16%	5.19/1	1
2. Has the lowest prices (9% of sample)....	81	19	4.26/1	2
3. Has the most courteous, friendly staff (40% of sample)............	75	20	3.75/1	3
4. Has the best quality private label brands (32% of sample)........	67	24	2.79/1	4
5. Has the fastest checkout counters (37% of sample)............	65	24	2.71/1	5
6. Has the best weekly "specials" (37% of sample)............	65	24	2.71/1	6
7. Has the best overall customer service (49% of sample)............	64	24	2.67/1	7

80

TABLE 15 (CONT'D.)

| AMONG THOSE WHO SAY PUBLIX............ | What Percent Shop Publix | | Ratio: Shop Most Often/ Shop Second Most Often | Rank |
	Most Often	Second Most Often		
8. Is the best at being in-stock with items they need (45% of sample)............	65%	26%	2.50/1	8
9. Has the best quality meat (43% of sample)................	56	25	2.24/1	9
10. Has the best overall assortment of non-food merchandise (19% of sample)........	61	28	2.18/1	10
11. Has the most pleasant shopping environment (51% of sample)...........	58	27	2.15/1	11
12. Has the best variety/assortment of meat (44% of sample)................	55	26	2.11/1	12
13. Has the cleanest stores (60% of sample)	52	25	2.08/1	13
14. Has the largest overall assortment/ variety of food products (49% of sample)	56	28	2.00/1	14
15. Has the best overall advertising (50% of sample)................	53	30	1.77/1	15
16. Has the best quality produce (55% of sample)................	49	32	1.53/1	16

81

TABLE 15 (CONT'D.)

AMONG THOSE WHO SAY PUBLIX............	What Percent Shop Publix		Ratio: Shop Most Often/ Shop Second Most Often	Rank
	Most Often	Second Most Often		
17. Has the best specialty baked goods department (57% of sample)............	48%	32%	1.50/1	17
18. Has the best delicatessen department (63% of total sample).............	45	31	1.45/1	18
19. Has the highest prices (66% of sample)	27	30	0.90/1	19

*READ: In the total sample of 1,000 respondents, 27 percent said Publix was the easiest store to get to from their home. Of that group, 83 percent also shop Publix most often and a further 16 percent shop Publix second most often. Thus, location is a good lever in attracting more customers and it works best in attracting primary rather than secondary shoppers. You push that lever by building more stores.

TABLE 16

RELATIVE FREQUENCY OF CHOICE VECTORS FOR INDIVIDUAL SUBJECTS
COMPUTED FROM CATSUP PURCHASES OVER TWO PERIODS
THREE YEARS' DURATION 1960-62 AND 1963-65

SUBJECT/TIME	Share of Purchases Going To Three Most Frequently Purchased Brands			Proportion of Total Catsup Purchases
	1st	2nd	3rd	
310, 1960-62	34%	16%	12%	62%
310, 1963-65	33	17	16	66
367, 1960-62	32	32	12	76
367, 1963-65	64	18	2	84
677, 1960-62	54	17	13	84
677, 1963-65	32	31	26	89
842, 1960-62	29	25	21	75
842, 1963-65	29	24	14	67
1012, 1960-62	92	8	0	100
1012, 1963-65	96	4	0	100
1511, 1960-62	65	8	6	79
1511, 1963-65	68	19	5	92
1623, 1960-62	100	0	0	100
1623, 1963-65	93	6	1	100
1637, 1960-62	88	7	5	100
1637, 1963-65	79	12	5	96
1895, 1960-62	100	0	0	100
1895, 1963-65	100	0	0	100
2045, 1960-62	60	20	10	90
2045, 1963-65	50	32	14	96

Source: Bass, 1978

is no different from what can be observed about brand
buying behaviour. Table 16 reports on a few subjects
from the Bass [2] review paper on brand choice as a
stochastic process. Not only did most subjects concentrate their purchasing in two or three brands over
long periods of time, the degree of concentration
rose in the second time frame compared to the first
time frame. Most consumers have a small evoked set
for both brand and store choice in the grocery arena.
The game may well change as consumers move from low
to high involvement product classes such as fashion.

CONCLUSIONS

After seven years of research, what are the key conclusions about consumer behaviour in general, attribute importance, determinancy, and store performance for food shopping?
First, the critical store attributes are location, price, assortment, service and cleanliness. Second, chains that dominate the market on all five varibales always do well. Third,
chains that dominate on some, but not all of the five can still
do well if they are within some acceptable threshold level on
others. Publix has a high price image in TSP but still has the
best market performance. If it was out of line by six or seven
percent on price, its only weak dimension, it would lost many
of its current customers. Fourth, attribute importance ratings
differ widely across markets and across shoppers of different
chains in the same markets. Fifth, the leverage factors (the
hot buttons) for each chain are different. If they improve
on the wrong dimensions, they will experience no improvement in
market performance. Finally, the acceptable set of stores for
each consumer is highly constrained by location and is in
general a set of only two or three stores. The store choice
process is not much different from the brand choice process.
Only the critical attributes are different.

REFERENCES

1. Alpert, Mark I. "Identification of Determinant Attributes:
    A Comparison of Methods," Journal of Marketing Research, 8
    (May, 1971), 184-91.

2. Bass, Frank M. "Analytical Approaches in the Study of Pur-
    chase Behaviour and Brand Choice," in Selected Aspects of
    Consumer Behaviour. Washington: National Science Founda-
    tion, 1978.

3. Coombs, C.H. A Theory of Data. New York: Wiley, 1964.

4. Fishbein, Martin. Readings in Attitude Theory and Measure-

ment. New York: Wiley, 1967.

5. Granbois, Donald H. "Shopping Behaviour and Preferences,"
    in Selected Aspects of Consumer Behaviour. Washington:
    National Science Foundation, 1978.

6. Hansen, Fleming. "Psychological Theories of Consumer
    Choice," in Selected Aspects of Consumer Behaviour. Wash-
    ington: National Science Foundation, 1978

7. Huff, D.L. "A Probalistic Analysis of Consumer Spatial
    Behaviour," in W. S. Decker (ed.), Emerging Concepts in
    Marketing. Proceedings of the Winter Conference of the
    American Marketing Association, Chicago, 1962.

8. Sethi, S., Caines, P. and C. W. Keng. "A Bivariate Econo-
    metric Analysis of Supermarket Sales," unpublished working
    paper, Faculty of Management Studies, University of
    Toronto, 1978.

9. Tigert, D.J., Cotter, T. and S. Ma. Mom Always Liked
    Ralph Best: The Strategic Crisis for Safeway in California,
    University of Toronto, 1976.

10. Tigert, D.J. and Bert Willems. The Amsterdam West Super-
    market Industry: Consumer Attitudes Towards and Shopping
    Habits At The Major Food Chains, University of Toronto,
    1978.

11. Tversky, A. "Elimination by Aspects: A Theory of Choice,"
    Psychological Review, 79 (July, 1972), 281-99.

12. Wilkie, W.L. and R.P. Weinreich. "Effects of the Number
    and Type of Attributes Included in an Attribute Model: More
    Is Not Better," in M. Venkatesan (ed.), Proceedings of the
    Third Annual Conference of the Association for Consumer
    Research, 1972, 325-40.

MATCHING ATTITUDE STRUCTURE TO MARKET STRUCTURE

James H. Myers[1], University of Southern California

INTRODUCTION

While a great deal of work has been done to analyze the structure and composition of attitudes, very little thought has been given to how these factors relate to the context within which attitudes operate. Most of the discussion to date has dealt with the structure of "an attitude toward an object" without specifying anything about the type of object, the circumstances under which an evaluation or choice is to be made, the nature of the constituent attributes of the object to be evaluated, or other considerations.

The purpose of this paper is to discuss some of these considerations, to review the limited available evidence as to their effects upon attitude structure, and to speculate about possible additional effects that have not as yet been subjected to research investigation.

Before doing this, however, it would be well to review briefly the major types of attitude models that compete against one another. Some are well known, but others are relatively obscure, to say the least. Because research to date has usually focused on analyzing "an attitude toward an object," the alternative models are currently considered to compete against one another. Complementarity has rarely been considered. In other words we have usually asked the question, "Which attitude model is most accurate?" rather than asking, "Which attitude model is most appropriate within a given evaluative context?"

OVERVIEW OF ATTITUDE MODELS

When we talk about attitude models, we are talking essentially about a way of describing the structure or composition of attitudes toward an object, a person or an idea. Now, any kind of model in the social sciences consists of two components: variables and relationship. In the case of attitude models, the variables are different types of respondent ratings of the attributes of the object, person or idea, and the rela-

---

[1]The writer wishes to thank James R. Bettman and Richard J. Lutz of the UCLA Graduate School of Management for help in the preparation of this manuscript.

tionships show how these different types of ratings combine to produce an overall evaluation. The objective is to evaluate or choose among objects on the basis of their component attributes or features.

For each of these attributes there are several things we want to know: how much of the attributes does each object possess (referred to as "belief"), is the attribute good or bad ("evaluation"), how important is the attribute in shaping overall attitude or affect ("importance"). If we secure respondent ratings on each of these factors (or on beliefs and importance only, since the goodness or badness of the attribute is often obvious) we can study different ways of combining them to determine the best form of relationship for predicting overall evaluations most accurately. The result is that we have specified the variables and relationships in an attitude model.

It is important to note that there are two alternative approaches to constructing an attitude model. The most obvious approach is to ask respondents for direct ratings of beliefs, evaluations and importance and then to combine the resulting ratings in different ways until we find the best prediction of overall evaluations. This is known as the "composition" approach.

In contrast, the "decomposition" approach asks respondents to give beliefs ratings only or to give no ratings at all but to simply judge how similar or dissimilar each object or person is to every other object or person. The resulting ratings or judgments are analyzed by any of several different statistical methods (non-metric multidimensional scaling, correlation analysis, etc.) to determine what beliefs, evaluations and importance values would best reproduce overall evaluations of the objects or persons. Some of the analytic methods can be used for only a single respondent (individual-level analysis), and some can be used at both levels.

The Basic Multi-Attribute Attitude Model

With the above preliminary comments out of the way, let us proceed to a review of the major competing attitude models. Most of these encompass many attributes or features of an object (multi-attribute models), others consider only a single feature or the object as a whole. First, a brief review of the voluminous literature on a particular form of multi-attribute model that has received the most attention to date. This is referred to as either the Rosenberg/Fishbein or the adequacy-importance model. It is technically a "weighted linear compensatory" model. The formulation is:

$$A_{jk} = \sum_{n=1}^{n} I_{ik} B_{ikj}$$

where

A_{jk} = <u>overall</u> attitude evaluation score of brand j for respondent k

I_{jk} = <u>importance</u> weight for attribute i

B_{ijk} = <u>belief</u> of extent of attribute i in brand j

i = attribute

j = brand

k = respondent

Note that this is a <u>weighted</u> model in the sense that beliefs ratings are weighted by their respective importance, <u>linear</u> in the same sense that none of the ratings is raised to any power, and <u>compensatory</u> because a high score on one attribute averages out a low score on some other attribute. Thus, weakness on one or two attributes of a product can be offset by strength on others.

A great deal of research has been done to explore systematically the best ways of operationalizing this model. Most of this work was reviewed in an excellent article by Wilkie and Pessemier [22]. Such issues as the following have been explored in some detail: how many attributes are needed, how can we be sure that all important attributes have been included, which attributes are most important, how should beliefs, evaluations and importance be measured, are importance weights needed at all, does standardizing ratings improve the accuracy of the model, how should ideal points or levels be determined for each product characteristic (such as sweetness, carbonation), what is the best structure for the model (multiplying vs. adding component ratings, raising components to higher powers, etc.) and many other issues.

To even summarize all of the above work would require much more time than is available. Suffice to say that we know a great deal about how to operationalize the Rosenberg/Fishbein, adequacy/importance attitude model and about the structure of this type of model. While all of this work has been very useful in helping us understand attitudes much better than we did 10-15 years ago, it occurs to me that we may have spent too much time on only a single form of attitude model when we should, instead, have done more to compare this form against

88

other forms under a variety of conditions. Had we done this we would know a great deal more about the subtle complexities of attitude structure and composition than we do now, in my opinion.

Other Types of Models

Several other types of attitude models have been studied in the marketing literature but few of these have been examined very thoroughly or compared with the basic model under a variety of conditions. Many have not even been operationalized in a more or less standard fashion, at least in the marketing literature.

Lexicographic. This rather imposing term refers to the simple idea that people evaluate or choose among objects on the basis of only the single attribute they feel is most important. Thus, if gas mileage is the most important consideration in small cars for a particular individual, he/she will choose the car that has the best gas mileage; if two or more cars get about the same mileage, the individual chooses the car that is best on the attribute that is next most important to him/her (e.g., styling), and so on. The price conscious consumer is using a lexicographic model -- "buy the cheapest." Note that this model does not provide an overall evaluation for all competing alternatives; it is only a choice model and it is non-compensatory.

There is some recent evidence in favor of the lexicographic from a proprietary study of airline travel that was done by a friend of mine. Respondents were asked which airline they would choose if scheduling were the same to a given destination. They were also asked to rank in importance the various attributes of airline travel and to rate several airlines on each of these attributes. Results showed that the most preferred airlines could be predicted correctly for 85% of respondents based on the single attribute they considered most important. For example, nearly all people who said food was most important to them chose a certain airline, those who felt that friendly employees were most important chose another airline, and so on. This study plus some others provides strong support for the notion that a simple lexicographic model may be quite adequate to explain overall preferences in some situations at least [24,25, 26].

Lexicographic Semi-Order. This is a modification of the lexicographic model which requires that the brand rated highest on the most important attribute be "significantly" or noticeably higher than other brands on this attribute. Other than this requirement, the consumer proceeds as in the lexicographic

89

model [13, 15, 19].

Conjunctive. This model proposes that people evaluate objects or people by setting a minimum standard of acceptability on each attribute and eliminating objects that do not measure up to this level on all of the attributes being measured. The individual considers all objects in some unspecified sequence and rejects those that are critically deficient on one or more attributes [4, 5, 6, 12, 14, 15, 23].

Thus, one shampoo might be rejected because it did not leave the hair squeaky-clean, another because it did not smell good enough, another because of too little lather, and so on. If more than one shampoo passes the minimum standards on all attributes, the way consumers make the final choice has not been clearly specified for this model. Some researchers believe one thing, others believe another.

Note the contrast between this model and the compensatory model (Rosenberg/Fishbein). The latter allows strength on one attribute to compensate for weakness on another; the conjunctive model does not -- it proceeds by elimination, in effect. Just how this would work is a matter of some controversy. Some say it is an additive process, others say it is a sequential process. It seems clear that we need to operationalize the conjunctive model more consistently and to compare it to the compensatory model more carefully under several conditions.

Disjunctive. The disjunctive model is the opposite of the conjunctive. Alternative products are considered acceptable only when they are perceived to be clearly superior on one or more attributes. Evaluation proceeds by looking at products' best features rather than their worst, as in the case of the conjunctive model. Like the conjunctive model, the disjunctive model may also result in several objects being judged as acceptable (because they are superior on one or more attributes) and it is not clear how the final choice is made when this is the case [4, 5, 6, 12, 23].

Sequential Elimination/Elimination by Aspects. These are more general forms of the elimination process specified by both conjunctive and disjunctive models. They propose that consumers proceed by examining all objects on one attribute at a time. The order in which the attributes are considered is not specified in the case of the Sequential Elimination model; in the Elimination by Aspects model attributes are assumed to differ in importance and the most important attribute is examined first, the second next and so on. Here, again, it is not clear how the final choice is made if more than one object or person survives the screening on all attributes [20,21].

Phased Models. These models propose that the consumer proceeds through the evaluation process in steps or phases. One attitude model might be used in the first phase, another in the second, and so on. For example, an elimination-type model might be used in the first phase and the objects that survive this screening might be evaluated by a compensatory or lexico-graphic model in the second phase. These models have a great deal of intuitive appeal and would seem to offer considerable promise for higher-priced, higher-involvement types of prod-ucts/services of some complexity [8, 14, 15, 17, 18, 24].

Thus, a great variety of attitude models are available to choose from. And if the above models are not to your liking, there are others: Affect Referral, Additive Difference, Gen-eral Information Integration, etc., etc. Or, you can invent your own. It's open season on attitude models!

This makes it especially difficult to answer the question as to which of these models is the most accurate. Several of the studies referenced above have compared 3-5 of these models against one another in different contexts. Results have not been conclusive, to say the least, but there is some support for the contention that the compensatory model is as good or better than most other models under most conditions. However, this has by no means been clearly established.

My own answer to the question as to the best model is: none of them -- all of them -- it depends upon the context. I personally would be quite surprised if we found that a single model were found to be superior under all conditions. What is needed is much more work to determine the various factors that affect the suitability of attitude models in a wide variety of contexts, and which types of models tend to be best under which types of conditions.

FACTORS DETERMINING APPROPRIATE MODEL

It seems to me that there are at least four major types of factors that affect or determine what type of attitude model would be most appropriate for a given situation or context. These factors are:

-- the individual
-- the task or choice situation
-- market structure
-- attribute structure.

There is evidence in the literature to support most of these; the others reflect speculation based on my own research.

Individual Factors

The notion that people have their own idiosyncratic evaluation styles draws its primary support from some work by Bettman, Capon and Lutz [3]. They proposed the term "cognitive algebra" to reflect the different ways (models) people have for combining attributes into an overall evaluation or effect. In one task situation they found that some people used an adding model (adding together beliefs and importance ratings for a given attribute rather than multiplying, as proposed by the Rosenberg/Fishbein model), some used a unipolar or bipolar multiplying model, others used an asymmetric multiplying model, a curvilinear multiplying model and so on.

Just how pervasive these idiosyncracies are we do not know from a single study, of course. If they turn out to be completely dominant, which is unlikely, they would obviate consideration of the other factors I proposed above -- or any others, for that matter. This is a fertile area for additional research, and it should receive high priority in my opinion.

Task or Choice Situation

Some recent work suggests that several aspects of the situation or context have an effect on the form of attitude model people use; e.g., the time available, format in which the information is presented, number of objects or people to be evaluated, the a priori degree of knowledge about the alternatives, and many other factors.

In the case of time available, there is some evidence that under great time pressure people tend to overweight negative information -- especially when effects are expected to come sooner rather than later. Also under time pressure, people tend to dichotomize attributes. Instead of trying to scale them in the usual way, they simply decide whether an object or person is acceptable or unacceptable on each attribute [27].

The format in which information is presented includes several factors. For example, as the number of objects or people to be evaluated increases, people tend to move toward phasing models. In evaluating a large number of competing snack foods, for example, they might use elimination models first and then a lexicographic or compensatory model. Also, as people are given too much information of an extraneous nature, or if information is presented in different formats for each object, people tend to move away from compensatory models and toward simple ones like the lexicographic [23, 24]. Another study found that when respondents had a high degree of prior familiarity with the product class they tended to use a compensatory model, but when

92

their prior familiarity was only moderate they tended to use conjunctive and disjunctive models [12].

These are but a few of the many task/environment effects that have been found to influence choice of attitude model. There seems to be much more evidence in the literature about these types of factors than for any of the other types I have chosen to discuss today.

Market Structure

The third type of factor affecting choice of attitude model includes those relating to market structure. Very little has appeared in the literature to date about the relationship of attitude structure to market structure. Ed Tauber and I wrote a book entitled Market Structure Analysis that was recently published by the American Marketing Association [11]. In that book we discussed several types of market structure, some of which are relevant to our discussion this morning.

One popular approach to structure is the use of positioning maps. It is not very widely known that there are two major competing types of maps: perceptual and preference. Perceptual maps show how people distinguish among products/brands in a given category, preference maps show how people evaluate these products/brands in relation to features considered most important. I personally believe that most of the perceptual maps that are built should be preference maps instead -- but that's another matter.

In any event, there are several ways in which knowledge of market structure through positioning maps can strongly suggest the most appropriate type or types of attitude models. For example, a perceptual map of only two dimensions says that only two major types of attributes (in the principal components sense) appear to distinguish among the products/brands in a category (this is often found to be the case). This suggests that we need only a two-attribute attitude model or less (since one of the two might not even be very important in evaluating the products/brands). The remaining attributes need not be included in the model because even though they are important, they cannot influence overall evaluations to any meaningful extent since they are not appreciably different among the competing products. This is the concept of "determinant attributes" which states that an attribute must be important and must differ noticeably among competing offerings if it is to have any effect upon choice behavior [10].

Similar comments can be made about preference maps, except that these maps indicate directly how many factors (dimensions) are important in evaluating products/brands -- the very information we need for constructing an attitude model. Moreover, they tell us the relative importance of each of the major attributes. And, both types of maps indicate how the separate attributes relate to one another and how they group together into "major factors" (i.e., principal component dimensions). All of this offers clear guidance in suggesting whether we need a simple or complex model, a single vs. a phased model, etc.

Another aspect of market structure is the general type of product or service to be evaluated. Presumably low-priced packaged goods sold in a store would require a different type or types of models than large appliances, automobiles, or homes. The latter objects would almost certainly involve the consideration of many more attributes, certainly the risk or involvement would be higher, the purchase time span greater, and so on.

Even packaged goods would be expected to differ in terms of appropriate models. A simple lexicographic model is probably all that is necessary for such items as insecticides (kills the most bugs) or peanut butter (tastes best) while more complex models might be needed for frozen packaged dinners or cold cereals paks. Some work has been done in this area, but we need to do much more.

Another area where some work has been done is the matter of consumption situation. Several studies have shown that the situation or circumstances under which a product is consumed can have a decided effect upon the product selected for self-consumption [2, 9, 16]. Kakkar and Lutz studied three alternative approaches in an effort to develop some sort of general taxonomy or classification scheme for consumption situations [7]. To date we have no such scheme but we do have ample evidence that product-specific situation taxonomies can be developed and that these affect choice among competing products/brands and hence, presumably, the most appropriate type or types of attitude models.

I was personally involved in a very large proprietary study of the entire beverage market -- seven billion drinks a year. We measured a great many aspects of each separate beverage consumption; among these was the situation the person was in -- what was he/she doing -- before, during, and after the beverage was consumed. We found it was relatively easy to develop a classification scheme for situations in which beverages are consumed. This work plus the many studies cited above suggest that it is quite possible to develop consumption situation taxonomies for many consumer goods. If this can be done then we can begin to systematically study how situation affects the type or types of attitude models that are most appropriate.

There are other aspects of market structure I feel might affect choice of attitude model: competitive structure for a given product category (e.g., one dominant brand vs. several), patterns of usage (e.g., complementarity among product categories) and perhaps others. To my knowledge no work at all has been done to study the ffects of these types of factors upon suitability of attitude models.

Attribute Structure

The last factor I feel would affect choice of attitude model is that of the nature or structure of the attributes used to describe the products to be evaluated. To my knowledge no one has pointed out in the marketing literature that the various words or phrases used for rating products are different from one another in some fundamental aspects that affect the way an attitude model should be operationalized. The discussion here is primarily in terms of the Rosenberg/Fishbein model.

In my own work I have come to distinguish four major types of attribute descripters:

Laboratory compounds/properties -- terms used by technical personnel to describe the ingredients or physical properties of a product.

Product Characteristics -- consumer terminology to describe the physical features of the product in objective terms.

Benefits -- statements telling what the product does for the consumer

Imagery -- what the product is felt to contribute to the consumer's self-image and/or what usage of the product implies.

Laboratory terminology needs no explanation. Product characteristics are descriptive aspects of the product itself (e.g., sweetness, thickness, carbonation) that people may or may not want or may want to very different degrees. Benefits are intrinsically desirable because they are what the product does for a person (e.g., cleans my hair, satisfies my thirst, tastes good). Imagery items are psychological associations that have been established in some way with the product (e.g., used by a rock star, an athlete, someone who is "with it"). Even though the criteria for distinguishing among these are not completely objective and measurable, it is usually not difficult to assign a given adjective or phrase to the appropriate grouping.

95

My own objectives have been to study the relationships among these four types of descripters for two purposes: 1) to understand how a given benefit or image (the real reasons why people buy products) can be delivered by technical personnel using laboratory compounds and processes, and 2) to trace the implications of the taxa in terms of how each should be operationalized in an attitude model.

To accomplish the first objective it may be possible to develop linkages which connect all four of the taxa, to show how a given image can result from (or at least be associated with) a given benefit(s), which in turn is produced by (associated with) a given product characteristic(s), and so on back to the constituent laboratory compounds/processes. Hypothetical linkages of this types are shown in Figure 1 for a women's shampoo and a liquid household cleaner.

This represents a process I call "benefit decomposition." Evidence from proprietary studies of my own (of the beverage market, and for both cooking sauces and sauces used at the table) shows that while relationship between benefits and product characteristics are rather low ($r \simeq .20 - .30$), multiple correlations would be high enough to offer meaningful guidance as to which product characteristics should be used (or avoided) to yield a given benefit.

These effects of attribute structure on attitude measurement are matters that seem to have been overlooked, in the marketing literature at least. In most empirical studies researchers have mixed two or even three of the attribute taxa into a single measuring instrument and have used the same scaling approach for all. My own position is that while the Rosenberg version of the compensatory model can be used for scaling benefits, images require the Fishbein approach (showing whether or not a given image is desirable) while product characteristics must be scaled by a tri-part model proposed by Ahtola which measures how much of a given attribute is wanted [1]. In my opinion, the differences among taxa are not trivial but rather are compelling in terms of choice of scaling method within any of the multiattribute models.

DISCUSSION

There may even be factors in addition to those above that affect choice of attitude model; for example, stage in the product life cycle. Early in the cycle there is little knowledge about the product category and very few competing brands -- perhaps only one in the beginning. At the end of the cycle there may again be very few brands, versus perhaps a large number of brands in the growth and maturity stages. Thus, simplistic mod-

96

FIGURE 1

BENEFIT DECOMPOSITION FOR WOMEN'S HAIR SHAMPOO AND LIQUID HOUSEHOLD CLEANSER

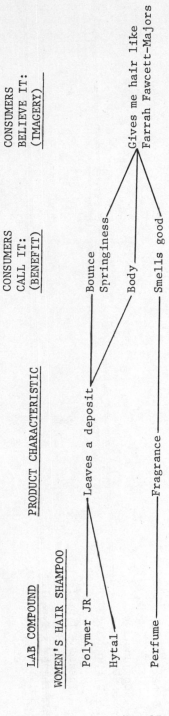
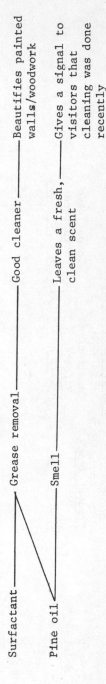

LAB COMPOUND	PRODUCT CHARACTERISTIC	CONSUMERS CALL IT: (BENEFIT)	CONSUMERS BELIEVE IT: (IMAGERY)
WOMEN'S HAIR SHAMPOO			
Polymer JR	Leaves a deposit	Bounce Springiness	Gives me hair like Farrah Fawcett-Majors
Hytal		Body	
Perfume	Fragrance	Smells good	
GENERAL PURPOSE LIQUID HOUSEHOLD CLEANSER			
Surfactant	Grease removal	Good cleaner	Beautifies painted walls/woodwork
Pine oil	Smell	Leaves a fresh, clean scent	Gives a signal to visitors that cleaning was done recently

97

FIGURE 2

ATTITUDE MODEL MATRIX

Type of Model	Product Type			Consumption Situation			Competitive Structure			etc.
	A	B	C	A	B	C	A	B	C	etc.
Rosenberg										
Fishbein										
Tri-part										
Lexicographic										
Conjunctive										
Disjunctive										
Phased – Type I										
Phased – Type II										
etc.										
etc.										

98

else would be appropriate at the beginning and end of the cycle, complex and/or phasing models during growth and maturity phases.

Of course, this type of speculation can go on and on. The obvious point is that at this time we have very little information about the various types of factors that dictate the appropriate form of attitude model and the best way of operationalising the chosen model. The only sensible conclusion is that no single model, or even general type of model, can possibly be appropriate for all choice or evaluation contexts.

Perhaps we will eventually have some sort of "model matrix" which shows for any specified context the type or types of models that would likely be most appropriate. Figure 2 shows how this might be done. Or, perhaps some clever analytical mind will come up with a "universal model" whose parameters are specified in such a way as to make it possible to shift from one model form to any of the others by simply specifying coefficients, exponents, term groupings, or even structural relationships in prescribed ways.

For the present we at least need to be aware of the various types of models that do exist and have been tested to some extent. And instead of trying to determine "which model is best" we need to shift our efforts to: 1) define more clearly the various factors that affect choice of attitude model, 2) develop clear and accurate taxonomies for these factors, 3) compare the various models under each of the types of choice contexts. If we do these things we will greatly improve the utility and applicability of attitude models over the next 5-10 years.

REFERENCES

1. Ahtola, Olli T. "The Vector Model of Preference: An Alternative to the Fishbein Model," Journal of Marketing Research, 12 (May, 1975), 52-59.

2. Belk, Russell W. "An Exploratory Assessment of Situational Effects in Buyer Behavior," Journal of Marketing Research, 11 (February, 1974), 156-163.

3. Bettman, James R., Noel Capon and Richard J. Lutz. "Cognitive Algebra in Multi-Attribute Attitude Models," Journal of Marketing Research, 12 (May, 1975), 151-164.

4. Bruno, Albert V. and Albert R. Wildt. "Toward Understanding Attitude Structure: A Story of the Complementarity of Multi-Attribute Attitude Models," Journal of Consumer Research, 2 (September, 1975), 137-145.

5. Einhorn, Hillel J. "The Use of Nonlinear, Noncompensatory Models in Decision Making," Psychological Bulletin, 73 (March 1970), 221-230.

6. Heeler, Roger M., Michael J. Kearney and Bruce J. Mehaffey. "Modeling Supermarket Product Selection," Journal of Marketing Research, 10 (February 1973), 34-37.

7. Kakkar, Pradeep and Richard J. Lutz. "Toward a Taxonomy of Consumption Situations," in Edward Mazze, ed., Combined Proceedings of the American Marketing Association, 1975, 206-210.

8. Lussier, Denis A. and Richard W. Olshavsky. "An Information Processing Approach to Individual Brand Choice Behavior," paper presented at ORSA/TIMS Joint National Meeting, San Juan, Puerto Rico, October, 1974.

9. Lutz, Richard J. and Pradeep Kakkar. "The Psychological Situation as a Determinant of Consumer Behavior," in M.J. Schlinger, ed., Advances in Consumer Research, Vol. 2 (1975). Urbana: Association for Consumer Research, 434-453.

10. Myers, James H. and Mark I. Alpert. "Determinant Buying Attitudes: Meaning and Measurement," Journal of Marketing, 32 (October 1968), 13-20.

11. Myers, James H. and Edward M. Tauber. Market Structure Analysis. Chicago: American Marketing Association, 1977.

12. Park, C. Whan and Jagdish N. Sheth. "Impact of Prior Familiarity and Cognitive Complexity on Information Processing Rules," Communication Research, 2 (July 1975), 260-266.

13. Pollay, Richard W. "Only the Naive are Transitive Decision Makers," Journal of Business Administration, 2 (Fall 1970), 3-8.

14. Pras, Bernard and John O. Summers. "A Comparison of Linear and Nonlinear Evaluation Process Models," Journal of Marketing Research, 12 (August 1975), 276-281.

15. Russ, Frederick A. "Consumer Evaluation of Alternative Product Models," unpublished doctoral dissertation, Carnegie Mellon University, 1971.

16. Sandell, Robert G. "The Effects of Attitudinal and Situational Factors on Reported Choice Behavior," Journal of Marketing Research, 4 (November 1968).

17. Sheridan, John E., Max D. Richards and John W. Slocum. "Comparative Analysis of Expectancy and Heuristic Models of Decision Behavior," Journal of Applied Psychology, 60 (1975), 361-368.

18. Svenson, Ola. "Coded Think Aloud Protocols Obtained When Making a Choice to Purchase One of Seven Hypothetically Offered Houses: Some Examples," unpublished paper, University of Stockholm, 1974.

19. Tversky, Amos. "Intransitivity of Preferences," Psychological Review, 76 (January 1969), 31-48.

20. Tversky, Amos. "Elimination by Aspects: A Theory of Choice," Psychological Review, 79 (July 1972), 281-299.

21. Van Raaij, W. Fred. "A Contingency Approach to Consumer Information Processing," unpublished paper, Tilburg University, 1976.

22. Wilkie, William L. and Edgar A. Pessemier. "Issues in Marketing's Use of Multi-Attribute Attitude Models," Journal of Marketing Research, 10 (November 1973), 428-439.

23. Wright, Peter L. "The Harassed Decision Maker: Time Pressures, Distractions and the Use of Evidence," Journal of Applied Psychology, 59 (October 1974), 555-561.

24. Wright, Peter L. "The Use of Phased, Noncompensatory Strategies in Decisions Between Multi-Attribute Products," Research Paper 223, Graduate School of Business, Stanford University, 1974.

25. Wright, Peter L. "Consumer Choice Strategies: Simplifying vs. Optimizing," Journal of Marketing Research, 11 (February 1975), 60-67.

26. Wright, Peter L. and Frederic Barbour. "The Relevance of Decision Process Models in Structuring Persuasive Messages," Communication Research, 2 (July 1975), 246-259.

27. Wright, Peter L. and Barton Weitz. "Time Horizon Effects on Product Evaluation Strategies," Journal of Marketing Research, 14 (November 1977), 429-443.

28. Wright, Peter L. and Frederic Barbour. "Phased Decision Strategies: Sequels to an Initial Screening," in Martin K. Starr and Milan Zeleny, eds., Multiple Criteria Decision Making, North Holland/TIMS Studies in the Management Sciences, Vol. 6. Amsterdam: North Holland, 1977, 91-109.

ATTITUDE THEORIES OF THE FUTURE: TOWARD A

DYNAMIC THEORY OF ATTITUDE CHANGE

Joseph Woelfel, SUNY at Albany
Elyse Werner, Michigan State University

While the mainstream of attitude research has proceeded by and large independently of phsycial science, nonetheless the recurrence of terms drawn from physical science such as force, mass, acceleration, work, power, energy and the like provides some evidence of the potential usefulness of physical models for attitude research. While many theorists might resist the notion that human attitudes may be described or explained by physical models, nonetheless there remains an intuitive usefulness to such concepts as a "forceful" speaker, "massive" attitudes, "powerful" or "energetic" advertising campaigns, the "momentum" of a political candidate, or efficient employees who turn out a great deal of "work", perhaps even at an "accelerating" rate.

Even though useful, these concepts do not have the precise definitions in attitude research that they have in physical science, in spite of sporadic attempts to establish social and psychological theories on a physical basis. Although early efforts have not resulted in a marriage of physical and social science, it is fair to say that no empirical evidence has as yet unambiguously ruled out the possibility of such a merger. Moreover, developments in the technological and methodological apparatus of the attitude researcher along with fundamental redefinitions of the principles underlying physical science due to the 20th century give some reason to suspect that investigation into the relationship between physical methods and attitude theory ought to continue and perhaps increase. Chief among these developments have been the widespread adoption by attitude researchers of multidimensional scaling methods which correspond closely to the coordinate reference frames of mathematical physics, along with a fundamental rethinking of the basic premisses of physical theory particularly by relativity theorists like Einstein [5] and quantum physicists such as Bohr [1] and Heisenberg [9].

While not itself a formal theory, this essay represents an attempt to look ahead in an informal way toward a possible future for attitude research based on principles of modern rather than classical physical science. In the first section of the paper we will rely on a description of four principles of modern science provided by Born [2], and show how these principles have led to the existing physical definitions of concepts like distance, velocity, acceleration, force, mass, work, energy and power. In the second half, we will discuss how the combination of these same principles with variants of modern techniques widely used in attitude research (in particular, metric multi-dimensional scaling) can lead to similarly precise definitions of these concepts within the domain of attitude theory. Whether these concepts ultimately show the utility for attitude research that they have for physical science can only be answered by data yet to be taken, but it is our purpose here to establish the possibility and feasibility of such a program.

KINEMATIC PRINCIPLES

The kinematic principles are those principles which establish a framework for the description of phenomena. These principles have been discussed in great depth by many workers [5, 11, 12] but we rely here on the concise account due to the physicist Max Born [2]. Born describes three basic principles on which all physical description is thought to rest. He calls the first principle "objectivization" which "...aims at making observations as independent of the individual observer as possible." Thus science is a process which trespasses "on the limits of the domain of the human senses" by finding the means of establishing "a maze of cross-connections whereby the purely geometric structures, as given by vision or touch, are preferred because they are the most reliable ones," that is, those which would not be expected to be dependent solely on the individual observer.

The second general principle Born identifies is "relativization." This principle states that the definition of one concept can only be accomplished by comparison with some other arbitrarily designated concept. Thus, "as long as the earth was regarded as a flat disk, the "up-down" or vertical direction at a place on the earth was something absolute. Now it becomes the direction towards the center of the globe and thus (is) defined only relative to the standpoint of the observer."

The third principle which Born identifies is that of "empirical verification." This principle states that "concepts and statements which are not empirically verifiable should have no place in a physical theory." In essence, this principle states that if a phenomenon cannot be "seen" and seen more than once, it cannot be a part of scientific theory.

These three principles, objectivization, relativization and empirical verification, are basic to modern scientific inquiry. They are guidelines by which scientists construct modes of differentiating among concepts and among levels of attri-

butes of concepts. In essence, these principles form the criteria for the formulation of systems of acceptable scientific
measurement. And it is measurement which allows the scientist
to identify regularities in phenomena which, in the absence of
measurement rules, would be only simultaneous and undifferen-
tiated experience.

Measurement. At its foundation, the process of measurement consists of fixing a unit of measure and defining a rule
for comparing other phenomena to this unit. This unit is an
arbitrarily established "rod" against which the phenomena are
compared according to some rule. Born states:

> The phrase "a length of so and so many meters"
> denotes the ratio of the length to be measured
> to the length of a meter. The phrase "a time
> of so many seconds" denotes the ratio of the
> time to be measured to the duration of a sec-
> ond. Thus we are always dealing with ratios,
> relative data concerning units which are them-
> selves to a high degree arbitrary [2].

The identification of a unit of measure thus involves two processes: fixing the unit, and then establishing the rules by
which phenomena are to be compared to the standard unit. As
Born notes, in physical science, this rule is universally a
ratio rule. Thus each measurement can be considered a ratio of
the instance of the phenomenon to the arbitrary fixed unit,
with the number representing the "amount" of the unit exhibited
by the phenomenon.

Two types of measurement may be distinguished. Fundamental measurement "... is a means by which numbers can be assigned according to natural law to represent the property and
yet which does not presuppose measurement of any other variable.
A construct measured fundamentally possesses both operational
and constitutive meaning of and by itself" [14]. Examples of
fundamental quantities are distance and time. These quantities
are given in terms of subsets of themselves. Thus any length
is defined in terms of its ratio to some arbitrary standard
length, and time intervals are measured as ratios to some arbitrary interval of time.

In contrast to fundamental measurement is derived measurement. "Derived quantities are those whose defining operations
are based on other physical quantities" [8]. Examples of derived quantities are velocity, acceleration, force, mass, momentum, work, power and energy -- precisely the concepts we
wish to define here. Derived measurement consists of deter-
mining a ratio between two properties (rather than the ratio of

a property to be a subset of itself), where the ratio is then defined as the quantity of the property to be measured. For example, velocity is defined as the ratio of the interval moved over the interval of time within which the movement occurred, and density is defined as the ratio of the mass of a substance to its volume. As of 1958, Torgerson [14] argued that social science could be characterized by a virtually complete absence of properly derived variables.

In both types of measurement, the process of comparison of the phenomenon to an arbitrarily defined unit according to a designated rule remains the same. Basic to measurement is the establishment of ratios of one magnitude to another. Torgerson [14] said, "as a matter of fact, the term measurement is often restricted to these (interval/ratio) kinds of scales, both in the ordinary use of the term and in more advanced discussions of the topic."

The Reference Frame. Having fixed the unit and rules by which to compare phenomena to the unit, the principle of relativization and objectivization demand that a reference frame be established. Edwards [4] states the importance of the reference frame:

> Without a reference system, it is impossible
> to specify where (a) body is or how it may
> be moving. Positions and motions are relative
> matters. Whether a body is to be regarded as
> at rest or in motion depends entirely upon how
> the particular reference system is selected...
> We may say a person sitting in a street car is
> at rest. He is at rest with respect to the
> streetcar even though it may be in motion.
> While the car is in motion, the man is not at
> rest with respect to the ground. But even if
> the car had stopped, our statement of the con-
> dition of rest of the man must again be qual-
> ified if we are to include a consideration of
> the earth's motion. Certainly he is not at
> rest with respect to the sun...

The reference frame chosen determines the measured value of a quantity. Thus, the same quantity may be given different values depending on the frame of reference held by the observer. By specifying the frame of reference with sufficiently clear and agreed upon rules, the criterion of objectivization may be satisfied; that is, it is then possible, through discovery of appropriate transformations, to find those relationships common among observers and to parse out those which are idiosyncratic to the individual reference frame. The search for relationships

which are invariant over such transformation is part of the
process by which science achieves its principle of objectivization.

The influence of the choice of reference frame is illustrated in the contrasting prediction and explanation generated
by the Ptolemaic and Copernican system of astronomy. The
former assumed the earth's surface to be at rest and the eter-
nal basis of the universe [2]. Thus, location of astronomical
bodies was accomplished through knowledge of two angles: that
between the observer's line of vision to the star with respect
to the horizon, and that between the observer's line of vision
and another appropriately chosen plane. In this system, "scientific concepts were still being drawn from the abundance of
subjective data" available to human perception [2] and therefore extensions of the theory were limited. For example, "as-
tronomic space was not actually considered as an object for
geometrical consideration, for the orbits were (considered)
fastened like rings to crystal spheres, which, arranged in
shells, formed the sky" [2]. Within the Ptolemaic system, the
earth is held at rest and the stars and other celestial bodies
describe roughly circular orbits within the reference frame.

When the Copernican system was advanced the earth was rel-
egated to a satellite of the sun, and "all immediate sense impressions were to be regarded as deception, whereas immeasure-
able distances and incredible velocities were to represent the
true state of affairs" [2]. Within the Copernican reference
frame, celestial bodies remain relatively motionless while most
visible motion is attributed to the Earth.

Despite its lack of reliance on intuitive or readily observable relationships, this system was destined to be adopted.
Its acceptance was based not on its degree of "rightness,"
but rather on its simplicity. As Born states, the Copernican
"system explained in a simpler way the phenomena which the traditional world system was able to explain only by means of complicated and artificial hypotheses" [2].

Thus the choice of a reference frame not only determines
the measured value of a quantity, but is also a matter of arbitrary choice. The choice depends upon that which the observer wants to hold stationary relative to the reference frame as
well as simplicity and utility.

Having established a unit of measure, consensus rules for
its application, and a reference frame, it is now possible to
describe the change obtained in measures of the phenomena over
time. Such a system of measurement is called a kinematic system, as it allows the observer to examine the rate at which an

object changes position with regard to the reference system over time (i.e., velocity) or the change in the rate of change (i.e., acceleration). But such a system does not allow an explanation of what causes change in the obtained measures. To address the issue of the cause of change in motion a dynamic system must be developed.

THE INERTIAL PRINCIPLE

To establish a dynamic system, a fourth principle must be added to the three principles already presented: an inertial principle. This principle is a statement of what is considered the "natural" state of the system under observation; it defines what kinds of events need to be explained within the system. In the Ptolemaic system, as we have seen, fixing the earth at the center of the coordinate system resulted in large near-circular motions of the stars within the reference system. Appropriately, Greek scholars like Aristotle defined circular motion as the perfect form of celestial motion which did not require further explanation. Deviations from circularity, however, do require explanation based on this inertial premise, and thus the epicycles generated by many thinkers to explain the deviations from perfect circular motions. In a Newtonian system, uniform rectilinear motion is defined as the "natural" form of motion, and such motions when observed do not require explanation. Non-uniform motions, however -- accelerations -- do require explanation. Since the inertial principle defines what characteristics of the system are to remain invariant when the system is left alone, changes in these characteristics must imply that the system has not been left alone, that is, it has been exposed to some _force_.

The concept most central to dynamics is force. Force is "at root a technique for relating the environment to the motion of a particle" [8].

The most rudimentary force is the instantaneous force called "impulse." Impulse is defined as the quantity derived from the number of instantaneous or impulsive forces acting on a body within i/n units of time, where n is the number of such instances. The greater the impulse, the greater the deviation of the object from its "normal" course. If the chosen inertial principle is the principle of uniform recilinear motion (as in Newton's first law), then "(t)he effect of impulses consists of sudden changes of velocity which are in the ratio of the impulse that produce them" [2].

Force is given full meaning, however, by its inverse concept, _inertial mass_. Following the principle of relativization, inertial mass is defined comparatively as the ratio of impulse to velocity, i.e.,

$$m = J/a$$

where J = impulse
      a = acceleration
      m = inertial mass.

Another way of understanding mass is to view it as the inertial resistance of a body. The formula states that for the same object, an increase in impulse is accompanied by an increase in acceleration such that the ratio remains the same.

Two implications of this definition can be drawn. First, the unit of measure for mass is fixed; it is determined by the units used for impulse and acceleration. Second, as Born [2] states:

> In ordinary language the word mass denotes
> something like amoutn of substance or quan-
> tity of matter, these concepts themselves
> being defined no further. The concept of
> substance is considered self-evident. In
> physics, however, as we must very strongly
> emphasize, the word mass has no meaning
> other than that given by the formula (m = J/a).
> It is the measure of the resistance of a
> body to changes of velocity.

If the inertial resistance of a body, i.e., its mass, is multiplied by the velocity of the body, the obtained quantity is defined as the momentum(p) of the body. That is,

$$p = mv$$

where m = mass
      v = velocty
      p = momentum.

Similarly, the product of mass and the change in velocity (acceleration) of a body in motion must therefore be assumed to be the result of an impulse or force. Relating these four constructs (force, velocity, mass and momentum), which we should recall are the results of definitions rather than observations, we obtain the law of motion of dynamics, which states

> If a force K acts on a body, then the momentum
> p carried along by the body changes in such a
> way that its change per unit of time is equal
> to the force K.

Within this system of definitions, _power_ is defined as the product of the magnitude of the force operating on an object and
the distance that the object moves within a specified time unit.
Further, ignoring the time interval, the product of the force
and the distance through which the force operates is defined as
the amount of _work_ done by the force. That is,

$$w = Kd$$

$$\text{and} \quad P = w/t$$

where K = force
d = distance
w = work
P = power
t = time

Energy as well may be given a constant definition within this
system as one half of the product of mass and velocity squared,
that is

$$E = \tfrac{1}{2}mv^2$$

This may be interpreted as the capacity of a particle of mass m
moving with velocity v to do work, or alternatively as the
amount of energy required to accelerate a body of mass m to a
velocity v from rest.

THE DYNAMICS OF OPINION

All this may seem at first to be just so much introductory
physics (and quite simplified at that) of no real relevance to
the attitude researcher. But the point of the first section
will be missed unless we understand that all the definitions
set down in the first half of the paper required no observations whatsoever, and are in fact consequences of the starting
principles and not of the subject matter. These definitions do
not describe physical reality, but rather the mode of theo-
rizing typical of the physical sciences. As such they are completely independent of the phenomena to which they are applied.
In the second half of the paper we will try to show how a consistent application of the principles of objectivization, relativization, and empirical verification, along with the stipulation of an intertial principle defined within a framework of
metric multidimensional scaling can be made to yield a dynamic
interpretation of attitudes and attitude changes. At the same
time we will try to establish procedures for giving unambiguous
and self-consistent definitions to an important set of derived
measures of potential usefulness to the attitude researcher,
including such concepts as velocity, acceleration, force, mass,

momentum, work, power and energy.

The reference frame. The principle of relativization, as
we have seen, states that a concept can only be defined by comparison with some other concept or concepts. This body of
"other concepts" with which the concept to be defined is to be
compared constitutes the reference system for the concept, and,
as Edwards suggests, "without a reference system, it is impossible to specify where (a) body is or how it may be moving" [4].
In the dynamical system sketched here, these other concepts may
be thought of as "landmarks" against which the position, velocity and acceleration of the concept of interest are to be
guaged. Market researchers particularly are familiar with
simple and reliable interview procedures by which the concepts,
attributes or issues in terms of which products, services, po-
litcal candidates or other objects are described. The principle concepts derived from procedures of this sort provide an
excellent starting point for establishing a reference frame for
a dynamic system of attitude measurement.

The standard measure. Once the set of reference objects
or landmarks has been selected, it is necessary to measure the
position of the landmarks relative to one another and the position of the concept of interest to the landmarks. Most commonly, the position of the product, service, candidate or other
concept of interest is measured relative to each of the land-
mark concepts by means of a category scale like a likert or semantic differential type scale, and the distances among the
concepts are then derived from the covariances or correlations
among these measures. Loss often the dissimilarities or distances are directly measured by a pairwize procedure, again
typically using a category type scale. The second procedure is
usually preferable to the first, since the errors around the
direct measurements will always be lower than the errors around
indirectly measured variables given scales of equal precision.
Nevertheless, neither method provides results optimal for our
present purposes as long as they are based on category type
scales, since the distances among the anchors on a typical category scale are themselves usually unknown. This results in a
kinematic system within which motions are complicated, and this
further complicates the process of establishing a dynamic system within the reference frame. Fortunately, however, substantial recent research has shown that scales of the exact type
described by Born [2] work quite well in the context of most
large-scale attitude research. Basically, as we have seen,
these scales require selecting the distance between any two of
the reference objects as a standard measure and expressing all
other distances as ratios to this standard. Research has indicated that excellent ratio level properties can be obtained by
this type of scaling on typical populations [7], and relative

errors of less than 10% at 100 cases are common in commercial practice, while experimental laboratory research has achieved relative errors of less than 1% under equivalent conditions. (The unfamiliar uses should be cautioned that standard and relative errors of these kinds of scales may not be compared directly with standard and relative errors computed for category type scales, since the less sensitive category type scales will necessarily yield artifactually lower error estimates when measuring identical variables due to the comparison of the tails of the distributions inherent in such scales.)

However measured, it is convenient to refer to the distances among these objects as "beliefs." If a concept of self is included in the set of reference concepts, it is convenient and useful to consider the beliefs which involve the self -- that is, the vectors from the self to each of the other concepts -- to be attitudes.

Mathematical coordinates. The attitude vectors can be given precise mathematical definition by means of classical metric multidimensional scaling procedures as defined by Young and Householder [16] and Torgerson [14]. Metric multidimensional scaling procedures have the effect of projecting the reference framework onto a mathematical cartesian coordinate system while preserving the interpoint distance relations among the concepts completely. We favor the metric procedure over the more recent non metric procedures first and foremost because they are most in keeping with the principle of empirical verification. Non-metric procedures all share as a common basis the assumption that the reference frame for all persons and for all groups of persons is or ought to be Euclidean, and violations of this assumption are transformed away by monotone iterative procedures. In our own work, however, as well as work by others, we find that the ratio pair comparison rule described above yields reliable violations of the Euclidean assumptions far too frequently to conclude that the Euclidean assumptions are viable [6, 16]. Metric procedures, on the other hand, when confronted by data of this type, produce higher dimensional Riemann spaces which have properties like those of the modern space-time continuum of relativity physics, which, of course, is also non-Euclidean.

The rotation rule. Within this coordinate system, concepts are located as position vectors from an arbitrary origin, and attitudes may be defined as vectors from the self concept to the remaining concepts. As is well known to psychometricians, however, when repeated measures are taken, the location of the origin and the orientation of the reference axes change except in the trivial case in which all measured values are scalar multiples of each other. Thus some scheme of rotation and translation is needed before relative changes among the concepts in the space may be measured. The choice of the rotation-translation rule determines completely the kinematics of the system. Many rotation schemes are available to the attitude researcher today [3, 13, 10], but the choice of an appropriate rotation and translation rule cannot be made on methodological grounds alone, since the choice of different rules leads to different values for measured motion within the framework. If we choose a rule, for example, which establishes the origin of the space on the self concept for every time period, then attitudes will be defined as position vectors from the origin. Within this space, all change of attitude will be seen as changes in the environment of an unchanging self, since the position of the self within the reference frame is fixed by the rotation rule. This is quite similar to the Ptolemaic view of celestial phenomena, and has similar theoretical consequences. On the other hand, if the origin of the space is situated at the centroid of a set of relatively stable concepts other than the self and the rotation rule attempts to minimize the positional changes of these stable concepts over time, changes in attitude will be attributed to the changing position of the self in a relatively stable set of reference concepts. We are free to choose any rule at all, of course, but the principle of objectivization requires that we choose a rule sufficiently explicit that any independent observer may use the rule unambiguously. Only observers who agree to abide by the same rule will observe identical outcomes.

Kinematics of attitudes. Once the rotation-translation rule has been agreed upon, the kinematics of the attitude system is established. Within the reference framework yielded by the rule, an attitude at any instant is given by the vector R, whose origin is the self concept and whose end point is the object of the attitude. Change in attitude is given by a change in the position vector, which we will symbolize as dR. The velocity (rate of change) of the attitude is given by the magnitude and direction of the change over time, or

$$V = dR/dt$$

where dt referes to the interval of time. Similarly, the acceleration of the attitude change at any instant is given by the second derivitative of the position vector,

$$a = d^2R/dt^2.$$

These concepts are well-defined and within the current technological capacities of attitude researchers. Moreover, they have predictive utility even without the additional steps re-

quired to establish a true dynamic model, since a kinematics
alone is sufficient to establish a statistical basis for projective forecasting based on accumulated observations over time.
Nonetheless, the derivation of what are usually called "laws"
within the reference frame depend on the stipulation of an inertial principle.

The inertial principle. As we suggested earlier, an inertial principle is a specification of what the "natural state"
of a system is taken to be when the system is not under the influence of external forces. In the Ptolemaic system of the
Greeks, where the earth was held fixed at the center of the
coordinate system, most heavenly bodies describe roughly circular paths around the earth each 24 hours. Within this system
it was convenient to choose an inertial principle which defined
circular motion as natural. This in fact was the choice of
Aristotle and most Greek philosophers. The notion that circular motion is the natural state of affairs means that only deviations from circular motion need to be explained. Within
this system, it is easy to see why the major work of Ptolemaic
astronomers was to find epicyclic models to account for the observed deviations from perfect circularity commonly noted.

In the Copernican system, on the other hand, where the
coordinate system is fixed against the stars, circular motion
is uncommon, and the most reasonable inertial principle is in
fact the first law of Newton: uniform straight line motion.
Based on this inertial principle, only deviations from rectilinear motion need to be explained. When a body (or an attitude) changes at a constant rate, no explanation is required.
When unifrom rectilinear motion is not observed -- that is,
when accelerations are noted -- then explanations are required.
Based on such a model, accelerations require the stipulation of
forces in the direction of the acceleration and proportional to
their magnitudes. Inversely, the concept of inertial mass is
defined as the resistance of a body to acceleration when under
the influence of forces. Inertial masses of attitudes can thus
be determined empirically by exposing them to fixed forces in
experiments; the ratios of their inertial masses will then be
well defined by the inverse of the ratio of their observed accelerations. Since momentum is given by the product of mass
and velocity, massive concepts moving at high velocities will
have high momentum, which is a precise formulation of the useful but imprecise notion of the momentum of a product or political candidate in the market or in an election campaign.
Similarly, when one works against opposing forces as is the
case when one tries to lift an object against the force of gravity or to elect a candidate against opposition forces, the
amount of work done can be precisely defined as the product of
the force expended and the distance through which that force

was expended. Following the same principles, the more power available, the smaller the time required to accomplish this work, and so effective power can be defined unambiguously as the amount of work done in a unit of time. Energy, similarly, may be defined as the capacity for doing work, and the amount of energy available will determine the amount of work to be done; conversely the amount of effective energy expended can be determined from the amount of work accomplished.

CONCLUSIONS

As we suggested at the beginning of this paper, the work reported here should not be thought of as a set of definitions ready to be put to use, but rather as a program of activities which can lead to such a set of definitions. Only the future can tell the extent to which such a campaign might be successful and useful. Nevertheless, a great deal of progress toward these goals has already been made. Relative (ratio) measurements have been used with good success both experimentally and in commercial practice. Metric multidimensional scaling programs have been in experimental use since the 1950's and have even made important penetrations into commercial work. Software for establishing alternative rotation and translation rules (such as the Galileo^{TM} metric scaling program) is both scientifically and commercially available. Experimental studies of the kinematics of metric multidimensional scaling spaces have appeared in the communication literature, and several such studies are in progress now. Procedures for defining optimal attitude change strategies based on the elementary kinematic principles described here have appeared in the communications literature [15] and these methods have also found important commercial applications in the last several years. While it would be rash to say, perhaps, that we are on the verge of a dynamic theory of attitudes, it is fair to say that a substantial part of the work prerequisite to such a theory has been accomplished and the prognosis for the future seems to be encouraging.

REFERENCES

1. Bohr, N. Atomic Physics and Human Knowledge, New York: John Wiley and Sons, 1958.

2. Born, M. Einstein's Theory of Relativity, New York: Dover, 1958.

3. Cliff, N. "Orthogonal Rotation to Congruence," Psychometrika, 31, 1966, 33-42.

4. Edwards, H. Analytic and Vector Mechanics, New York: Dover, 1965.

114

5. Einstein, A. _The Meaning of Relativity_, Princeton: Princeton University Press, 1974.

6. Gillnam, J., and Woelfel, J. "The Galileo System: Preliminary Evidence for Precision, Stability and Equivalence to Traditional Measures," _Human Communication Research_, 3, 1977, 222-234.

7. Gordon, T. "Subject's Ability to Use Metric MDS: Effects of Varying the Criterion Pair," Paper presented to the Association for Education in Journalism, August, 1976.

8. Halliday, D., and Resnick, R. _Physics_, New York: John Wiley and Sons, 1966.

9. Heisenberg, W. _Physics and Philosophy_, New York: Harper Torchbooks, 1958.

10. Lissitz, R.W., Scheremann, P., and Lingoes, J. "Solution to the Weighted Procrustes Problem in which the Transformation is in Agreement with the Loss Function," _Psychometrika_, 41(4), 1976, 547-550.

11. Mach, E. _The Science of Mechanics: A Critical and Historical Account of Its Development_, Chicago: Open Court Publishing Company, 1960.

12. Reichenbach, H. _The Philosophy of Space and Time_, New York: Dover, 1958.

13. Schonemann, P. "A Generalized Solution of the Orthogonal Procrustes Problem," _Psychometrika_, 31, 1966, 1-10.

14. Torgerson, W. _Theory and Methods of Scaling_, New York: John Wiley and Sons, 1958.

15. Woelfel, J., and Danes, J. "New Techniques for the Multidimensional Analysis fo Communication, Conception, and Change," in Monge, P., and Capella, J. (eds.), _Multivariate Techniques in Communication Research_, New York: Academic Press (forthcoming).

16. Young, G., and Householder, A. "Discussion of a Set of Points in Terms of Their Mutual Distances, _Psychometrika_, 3, 1938, 19-22.

THE COMPUTER AND THE CONTENT ANALYSIS OF QUALITATIVE RESPONSE: SOME POSSIBILITIES

G. Norman Van Tubergen
University of Kentucky

With varying degrees of enthusiasm or reluctance, most of the participants in this conference have made use of qualitative responses, the natural-language expression of attitudes as a necessary and useful part of the market research process.

Enthusiasm regarding qualitative responses arises primarily from their capacity to obtain data without imposing a limited set of answer categories. Of course, there would appear to be no alternative to natural language response in exploratory research such as focus analysis. When it comes to questionnaires, the respondent who is unrestrained by a pre-defined set of categories or scales can often provide unanticipated insights into a problem. In fact, the anticipated range of response might be so broad as to defy categorization in advance. Or, respondents might be expected to answer easily in very specific terms but find great difficulty in fitting their experience in to some more general categorical terms. And, there is some evidence to suggest that respondents are more satisfied when leaving a data gathering situation in which they have been allowed some opportunity for natural-language response.

Reluctance about the use of qualitative methods often arises from what happens after the data are gathered. Analysis may be highly impressionistic in nature. The development of categories and the coding of a few open-ended items for several hundred questionnaires often requires more time than the time required to keypunch and completely analyze all of the many structured items in the questionnaire -- and this comes at a stage of the project when time is at a premium. Despite all the sophisticated statistical tools available to the market researcher today for both description and inference (such as some of those being discussed at this conference), numerical analysis of qualitative data is usually limited to the most basic descriptions provided by categorical frequency counts and crosstabulations; one is sometimes left with the feeling that never has so much time and effort been invested for so little information return.

In short, most of the enthusiasm for the qualitative response arises from the information that it potentially can provide; most of the reluctance to use it arises when that potential is not realized due to a lack of rigor and/or sophistication in analysis. In this paper, I hope to show that this lack of rigor and sophistication need not prevail.

Of course, the kind of analysis we are talking about is content analysis for which there are some widely accepted methodological guidelines. Even though many of us are probably imlicitly aware of most of these points, I would like to review this methodology -- partly because a review can urge us to tighten up procedures we have allowed to become sloppy, partly because it will serve as background for some of what will follow, and partly because some aspects of the methodology may be fresh to some of you.

Following this, I would like to call your attention to some of the ways in which computers are used in content analytic work. To the best of my knowledge, computers have not been used to their fullest advantage for content analysis in the market research field. As is often the case, computers -- properly used -- hold great promise for improving both the rigor and the sophistication of the analysis of qualitative market data. In the last portion of my paper, I want to suggest one system (and its variations) which could be of substantial benefit to the researcher investigating market attitudes; what will be suggested is not something which exists, but something which could exist; it is not beyond the state of art, and in fact requires no accomplishments -- either hardward or software -- that are younger than five years old. But before we get to that, we review content analysis.

CONTENT ANALYSIS

In his 1952 classic and still-definitive work on content analysis, Berelson defined his subject in this simple way: "Content analysis is a research technique for the objective, systematic, and quantitative description of the manifest content of communication [1, p. 55]. Although other definitions have been offered in the past 25 years, this remains the most succinct identification of the elements of content analysis -- and one with which most will agree.

The Berelson definition pinpoints four elements in content analysis - objectivity, systematization, quantification, and manifest content; a fifth element, generalizability, is frequently mentioned by others [2, 7, 8] and is readily inferred from Berelson's discussion. The merit in three of these five points is that they are basic to the method of science. They stress that content analysis should not be a mere gathering of impressions through some subjective review of a corpus - regardless of the quality of those impressions.

117

The requirement that content analysis be <u>objective</u> specifically compels us to define our investigation with sufficient precision that other researchers using the same definitions could look at the same body of content and reach the same conclusions. Ordinarily, this means a careful definition of coding categories – one which leaves little margin for subjectivity in coding decisions. When we listen to tapes from a focus interview, draw subjective impressions, and then perhaps reach consensus in discussions with others working on the study, we may be reaching conclusions that are more closely related to ourselves as receivers than to the content of the messages on the tape; in this case, we are not adequately fulfilling the requirement of objectivity. When a team of questionnaire coders must frequently bring items to the project analyst and ask, "Where should I code this one?", the subjective coding interpretations made by one person are dominating the work. The implication is that there is a lack of precision in the coding categories, and while the results may be consistent, they probably do not meet the best standards of objectivity. (Measures of inter-coder reliability can be made as a check on objectivity; where the results from these tests are poor, efforts should be made either to improve coder training or to refine category definitions or both.)

But one might have a high degree of reliability, indicating objective coding, and yet have <u>systematic</u> bias. The second requirement is that categories for coding be formed according to a set of rules which will insure categories that reflect all pertinent message content. The exclusion of categories which would not support the researcher's hypothesis is a systematic bias. In market research applications, systematic bias seems to be less of a problem than lack of coding precision – although one does occasionally encounter the sentiment that there are some ideas in the data that we just "don't want to send on to the client."

Related to these first two, and also a basic notion in science, is the concept of generalizability. A datum should not exist in isolation, but should be fitted to some broader theoretical proposition by exploring relationships between it and other data. The crosstabulation of an open-ended question with other items in the questionnaire moves toward generalizability, though this tying-in is not as strong as it might be.

In day to day market research applications we can go a long way toward meeting these first three principles by defining categorical schemes for our content analytic work which are (1) stated in as precise a way as possible so that coding becomes a clerical task rather than a judgmental one, (2) are exhaustive of the content, (3) are mutually exclusive, and

(4) are representative of some body of theory.

   Of the other points in Berelson's definition, one that
raises some debate is the requirement that content analysis
focus on manifest content. Clearly, the requirement of objectivity demands that the coding process be limited to an examination of the literal content of the message itself. When it
comes to an interpretation of the data, there are two schools
of thought - which can perhaps be illustrated by two figures
from Budd, Thorp and Donohew's [2] book (although the figures
were intended to illustrate somewhat different points). These
illustrations place content analysis in the perspective of the
total communcation process. If we confine our interpretation
of the data to the manifest message -- the overt content -- we
look solely at the relationships internal to that part of the
communication process; that is, we focus strictly on the symbols in the message, their relationships to each other and to
the objects or states-of-being which they represent. An opposing view today is that our interpretations should take into account latent elements - factors that arise elsewhere in the
communication process which enrich the meaning of the manifest
content; here, for example, we add to the relationships found
in the manifest content, those relationships which we can infer
between the symbols of the message and its sender, or its intended receiver; in short, interpretation involving latent content is interpretation which "reads between the lines." It is
arguing to the effect: "Well, this is a bunch of housewives
saying thus-and-so -- or a bunch of corn farmers -- and therefore they probably mean such-and-such." Such assertions, if
based in a robust understanding of how housewives or corn farmers use language, can be quite valuable; made in a cavalier
manner, they detract from the scientific quality of the analysis. Ten years ago Mitchell [10] pointed out that developments being made in the fields of linguistics, sociolinguistics
and psycholinguistics held great promise for the development of
new and improved approaches to content analysis. The application of the burgeoning knowledge in these disciplines would be
of obvious benefit to those who would interpret latent content;
to date, however, few investigators outside of clinical set-
tings appear to have made serious attempts to follow Mitchell's
suggestion.

   The remaining element in Berelson's definition is quantification, and it has been held to the last because it might
jangle a few nerves: we are, after all, talking about qualitative data; how'd those darned numbers get in here again? Kassarjian [8, p. 9] calls quantification "the most distinctive
feature of content analysis" and argues that it "distinguishes
content analysis from ordinary critical reading." Let's quickly point out that Berelson did not mean that numbers were the

119

only kind of quantification possible. When you summarize a focus group session by saying, "they felt that the product's convenience was more important than its appearance," you have made a statement of quantification (however weakly defined). But by and large, that sort of quantification is what gives rise to the uneasy feeling that our analysis lacks rigor or sophistication. To improve on this situation, we resort to numbers, but it is our choices about what the numbers will represent and how we will treat the numbers subsequently which present the chance for stronger analysis.

As has been stated, we most often think in terms of forming some thematic categories and then marking the presence or absence of that category in the total verbal output of one respondent. Although they probably are the most obvious choice for attitude investigation, themes are not the only things the content analyst might look for nor is presence and absence the only way to assign numbers; and finally, the total verbal output of one respondent might not be the best unit to analyze. Time does not permit an exhaustive discussion of these points, but permit me a brief digression to offer a few illustrations.

Instead of enumeration at the thematic level, one could use the word as the basis for coding. Some rather psycholinguistic procedures are based on the word as unit, and these may have application to the analysis of latent content in the interview. For example, one can count the number of adjectives in a person's speech and form ratios with the number of verbs or nouns; schizophrenic personalities are known to use fewer adjectives, proportionately. The number of stress or discomfort words a respondent used can indicate how relaxed he or she felt in the interview. The type-token ratio is fundamentally a measure of vocabulary range and can help judge a respondent's adjustment of educational level.

As another example, we might abandon the total verbal output of one person as a coding unit when examining a lengthy group interview/discussion. Instead, we might tabulate themes by, say, five-minute time segments; this could reveal something about the structure of the attitudes present, as well as simply identifying them. Or the word-level analysis suggested a moment ago could also be carried out according to units of time or space, rather than people.

In short, by using different approaches to quantification, content analysis can serve many ends - very few of which have been explored by market attitude researchers. With rigorous content analysis of the verbal response, the use of projective tests could be much broader than it is: natural-language consumer diaries, properly and thoroughly content analyzed, could

offer a wealth of data. Before ending my digression, I would
like to share with you a chart designed by Holsti [6, p. 204]
which does an outstanding job of suggesting possible research
designs in content analysis. The chart is divided into three
major sections: the first poses questions related to manifest
content; the second proposes research problems that involve latent content in the sender-symbol relationship; and, the third
offers ideas involving the latent content in the receiver-sym-
bol relationship. The chart is further divided into the elements of Laswell's classic communication model: "Who says what,
to whom, how and with what effect?" The heart of the chart is
the far right-hand column, which lists a number of research applications:

- To describe trends in communication content
- To relate known characteristics of sources to mes-
  sages they produce
- To audit communication content against standards
- To analyze techniques of persuasion
- To analyze style
- To relate known characteristics of the audience to
  messages produced for them
- To describe patterns of communication
- To secure political and military intelligence
- To analyze psychological traits of individuals
- To infer aspects of culture and cultural change
- To provide legal evidence
- To answer questions of disputed authorship
- To measure readability
- To analyze the flow of information
- To assess responses to communication

As I look at Holsti's list, I see only two or three applications being widely used in the market research field; of
course, not all are appropriate, but I hope you'll agree there
are many more possibilities than are presently being explored.

But let's return to quantification of the sort most pertinent to our central concern this morning, the assessment of
attitudes. Again, we most commonly deal with thematic categories enumerated by their presence or absence. Typically, then,
we have a nominal scale that permits frequency counts and
crosstabulations (which is to say contingency analysis). There
is little more of possible use with nominal data. Occasionally
it is possible to establish an ordinal relationship in a set of
categories, which opens further possibilities. Often, we can
deal readily with attitude direction; that is, responses might
be easily coded as favorable, neutral, or unfavorable toward,
say, the client's product. In this case, we might use some
simple statistical procedures, such as Janis and Fadner's

121

[IN 2, p. 58] coefficient of imbalance.

When not working with natural language, we are much more accustomed to dealing with attitude data in numbers which we are willing to accept as an interval scale, with not only direction represented in the scale, but intensity as well. One set of content analytic procedures which results in this sort of data and which seems particularly well suited to investigations of attitudes in the marketplace is Evaluative Assertion Analysis [10]. Most content analysts agree that the strengths of evaluative assertion analysis are that it nearly eliminates subjective coding problems, it compels one toward a more generalizable view of the data and it provides interval-scale type values. In general it is seen as particularly suitable where very precise measures are desired regarding a relatively limited number of targets toward which attitudes can be directed; this would seem to describe the typical market research situation perfectly. Its main weakness -- and the major reason that it has been so little used since it was first described over twenty years ago -- is that the procedures are quite tedious and laborious; I hope to show a little later that I don't believe this weakness needs to be considered any longer.

An overview of Evaluative Assertion Analysis is in order. EAA deals with three elements in the manifest content. First is the Attitude Object; AO's are nouns or adjective-noun phrases which are relevant to the subject of investigation and about which differing evaluations are expected - for example, some feature of the client's product. The second element is the Common Meaning object (CM); these are also noun or adjective-noun phrases, but about which there is substantial agreement - for example, words like "the book" or "flavorful", and so forth. The third element is the Connector (C); connectors are verbs -- such as "hurt", "bend", or simply "are" -- which link an Attitude Object to another Attitude Object or to a Common Meaning object. When such a linkage is made, an assertion exists: "Starkist tuna has good taste." Ooops, sorry Charlie!

The analysis proceeds in the following steps: (1) The text in question is examined and all pertinent AO's are identified. (2) These AO's are masked by replacement with meaningless symbols which prevent coder subjectivity from entering later stages of the analysis. (3) All assertion in the text must be identified and isolated. If all messages were composed of simple declarative sentences such as the one about tunafish, this would present no problem; but real message texts are much more complex and require careful syntactic analysis. In their principal article about EAA, Osgood and his colleagues give extensive rules for the decomposition of text to assetions; more recently, Kimura [9] reduced the Osgood rules to 12 and summa-

rized them in a succinct and eminently useable chart form.
(4) Once isolated, assertions are entered into an EAA coding
form. On this form, column 1 is often used to identify the
message source when that is relevant. The second column is
used to list the masking code for the AO, for example "DK" or
"HG". The third column provides space to enter the connecting
verb phrase. The CM or second AO is listed in the fifth column. Columns four and six are completed in the next step.
(5) Once all the assertions have been transferred to the coding
form, a coder who is unfamiliar with the actual AO's represented by the masks -- or even the general topic of the research -- can objectively evaluate the direction and intensity
of the other elements in the assertions - "will not be" might
be deemed negative-2, "successful" could rate plus-3, and so
forth. (6) When values have been assigned to all assertions,
those assertions which reflect on a specific AO can be grouped
and the values summarized to a single evaluation score for that
AO on a seven-point scale. Of course, these values can be computed at whatever level desired - by individual source, say, or
across an entire group of sources. From this, the manner in
which all AO's were perceived by two different sub-populations
might be summarized in simple graphic terms; for example, President Nixon as an attitude object might be evaluated at +1 by
one source and at -2.4 by another. Other possibilities would
include using these scores in correlation, regression, factor
analysis - in short, they can be used in the same way as other
interval scale indices and can be modified and fitted to various attitude models.

THE ROLE OF THE COMPUTER

Computer can play two distinct roles in content analysis
work. The first is the role with which we are all most familiar - that of the number manipulator. The computer is properly
our high-speed clerk for generating frequency counts of numer-
ically-coded categories; it is, of course, the resource we
would turn to when applying correlation and other statistical
tools to such interval-scale data as might be developed through
Evaluative Assertion Analysis or other techniques.

The second role of the computer, and the one fewer of us
are familiar with in any detail, is that of symbol manipulator
- particularly a manipulator of the symbols of natural language. In this connection, probably the most widely known
software for content analysis is the General Inquirer system
[11], and now in its third or fourth major version.

The basic strategy employed by the General Inquirer is
simple, although actual execution can be quite involved.
First, the programs read the text to be analyzed into the ma-

chine. Each sentence of the text is isolated and the words in
the sentence are looked-up in a computer-resident dictionary;
the dictionary entry provides a "tag" or coding category which
is then associated with the sentence. The sentence is stored
with its tag or tags for subsequent analysis. Other programs
in the system will tabulate tags, generate concordances (that
is, retrieve all sentences for which a given tag occurs), and
perform a variety of other retrieval and tallying tasks.

What generally commends the General Inquirer system to the
content analyst is the fact that it is dictionary-driven. The
kinds of questions the researcher can ask depends upon the
kinds of tags provided in the dictionary. There have been several dictionaries created for the Inquirer over the years, and
if an existing one doesn't suit a researcher's needs, a new one
can always be added. The Third Harvard Psychosociological Dictionary, for example, classifies over 3500 words into fewer
than 100 tags relevant to psychological or sociological analysis of text; these tags include concepts such as "pleasure,"
"time reference," and "cultural deviation." There are dictionaries that are for anthropological concerns, for assessing a
person's need for achievement, and for political science application (one of which I will return to in a moment). Dictionaries of about 4000 words are usually adequate to recognize
over 95% of the words in typical text and to assign correct
meaning to these words about 95% of the time. Depending on the
nature of your study, one of the existing dictionaries might be
highly appropriate to your research; or perhaps it would be
valuable to develop a dictionary for general use in market attitude studies.

In order to identify the meaning of words correctly, some
of the dictionaries require knowledge of the grammatical classification of a word - noun, verb, adjective, and so forth.
Unfortunately, the versions of the system with which I am familiar contain no parsers; therefore, when this information is
needed, it must be coded into the text before input.

Computer parsing, of course, has obvious and far-reaching
advantages for content analysis by machine. Time does not permit extensive discussion; but it should be noted that in the
past 10 years or so, numerous parsing algorithms have been presented by researchers at MIT, IBM, Bell Laboratories, and elsewhere. Many of these algorithms successfully parse upwards of
75% or 80% of typical American conversational speech. Thus,
the major weakness in the General Inquirer is soluable.

Probably, the largest barrier to the use of computers in
content analysis where quantity of text is substantial is the
purely mechanical task of putting the text in machine-readable

form. In the past, we have thought solely in terms of endless keypunching. The prospects today, particularly for those in market research, look much brighter. Increasingly, data are being prepared on key-to-tape or key-to-disk equipment which is much more flexible than the keypunch. In some organizations, it is standard practice to transcribe group interviews from audio tape to typewritten document; if typed on a machine with an appropriate type face, that same document can be read by an optical scnner. The tremendous growth in WATS centers with interviewers recording data directly at an on-line computer terminal opens a wealth of possibilities for computer analysis of qualitative responses.

THOSE POSSIBILITIES

Which brings us to those possibilities mentioned in the title of this paper. In my concluding remarks, I'd like to borrow some bits and pieces from what has already been said to assemble a system I think you would like and find useful. Again, this does not exist, but it would take only money and effort to create; and it is not the only system one could propose - in fact, I hope that some of what I have said this morning might inspire you in different directions.

As attitude researchers, we are greatly attracted to Evaluative Assertion Analysis: it is particularly suited to generating precise information about the direction and intensity of feelings toward some specific small set of objects, it forces us to strengthen our objectivity, and it creates data that we will be inclined to use in more generalizable and sophisticated ways. It does, of course, involve a lot of clerical tedium. But that is what we have computers for! So let's base our hypothetical system on Evaluative Assertion Analysis.

The data are in from, say, your focus group; it has been typed up for the staff and the optical scanner to read; it is in the machine. Hit start! A parsing routine identifies the adjective-noun phrases. By reference to a dictionary, those which are common meaning objects are noted. Perhaps with some interactive prompting and verification by you, the analyst or project director, the Attitude objects are identified and replaced by arbitrary symbols; of course, a table of this information is retained but it need not, and probably should not, be displayed until analysis is complete. The parser has deduced the structure of each sentence and passes this information to a program which utilizes a series of syntactical rules (perhaps Kimura's) to decompose the sentence into one or more assertions.

At this point, the assertions in the text can be displayed, ordered by AO masking symbol, if desired. Several options occur. From an interactive terminal, the analyst might wish to carry out a manual tagging operation in which assertions are classified for simple tabulation; this would allow us to retain the specific qualitative character of the assertions in addition to direction and intensity measures. Or, the computer could do this categorized tagging using a General Inquirer-style dictionary' again, such a dictionary might be an existing one, a new one aimed at market research applications, or might even be one you have developed specifically for this client or product class. In any case, tabulated results are nearly immediate and interactive requests for crosstabulations with other elements in the data base are also answered promptly.

Let's continue with the EAA approach. Direction and intensity values can be manually assigned at the terminal to connectors and common meaning elements by the analyst, or (preferably) by some uninformed clerk, or possibly by some representatives from the target population. As in the previous case, a more interesting option is to allow the computer to assign the evaluation values. I mentioned a political science dictionary that is used with the General Inquirer. This dictionary recognizes between 3500 and 4000 words; each is tagged by its position in semantic space as identified over the years in semantic differential studies by Osgood and others. If you will recall Osgood's work, you will remember that he defines meaning in three dimensions - evaluation, activity, and potency. Unless it is neutral on a dimension, each word in the Stanford Political Science Dictionary is rated on an integer scale from +3 to -3 for each dimension. Thus, the imaginary system we are defining could make reference to this General Inquirer dictionary to find an evaluative score (and activity and potency scores as well) for the connectors and common meaning objects in the previously identified assertions. Items not in the dictionary might be resolved interactively by the analyst and later added to the dictionary. The system would then compute scores for each AO as seen by each person at our focus session; these could be related to other data available on each participant and comparisons among participants would be possible. Scores could also be aggregated for the group and so forth.

This, of course, is only a skeletal outline of one possible system. It cannot answer all questions and situations; and, if I have done my job, it has helped create in your mind more questions about the possibilities of computer-based content analysis for qualitative data than you had when we began. It is only through asking questions that we seek answers, changes, and improvements on our present methods.

REFERENCES

1. Berelson, B. <u>Content Analysis</u>. Glencoe, Ill.: Free Press, 1952.

2. Budd, R.W., R.K. Thorp, and R.L. Donohew. <u>Content Analysis of Communication</u>. New York: Macmillan, 1967.

3. DeWeese, L.C. "Computer Content Analysis of Printed Media," <u>Public Opinion Quarterly</u>, 40:1 (Spring, 1976), 92-100.

4. DeWeese, L.C. "Computer Content Analysis of 'Day-Old' Newspapers," Public Opinion Quarterly, 41:1 (Spring, 1977), 91-94.

5. Gerbner, C., O. Holsti, K. Krippendorff, W. Paisley, and P. Stone, eds., <u>The Analysis of Communication Content: Developments in Scientific Theories and Computer Technologies</u>. New York: Wiley & Sons, 1969.

6. Holbrook, M. "More Content Analysis in Consumer Research," <u>Journal of Consumer Research</u>, 4:3 (December, 1977), 176-177.

7. Holsti, O. "Content Analysis," in G. Lindzey and E. Aronson, eds., <u>The Handbook of Social Psychology</u>. Reading, Mass.: Addison-Wesley, 1968, Vol. 2, 596-692.

8. Kassarjian, H. "Content Analysis in Consumer Research," <u>Journal of Consumer Research</u>, 4:1 (June, 1977), 8-18.

9. Kimura, H. "Evaluative Assertion Analysis of Editorial-News Relationship," unpublished M.S. thesis, Southern Illinois University at Carbondale, 1972.

10. Mitchell, R.E. "The Use of Content Analysis for Exploratory Studies," <u>Public Opinion Quarterly</u>, 31:2 (1967), 230-241.

11. Osgood, C.E., S. Saporta, and J. Nunnally. "Evaluative Assertion Analysis," <u>Litera</u>, 41:3 (1956), 47-102.

12. Stone, P.J., D.C. Dunphy, M.S. Smith, D.M. Ogilvie. <u>The General Inquirer</u>. Cambridge, Mass.: MIT Press, 1966.

AN INVESTIGATION OF THE LEVELS OF COGNITIVE ABSTRACTION UTILIZED BY CONSUMERS IN PRODUCT DIFFERENTIATION

Jonathan Gutman, University of Southern California
Thomas J. Reynolds, University of Texas at Dallas

INTRODUCTION

As an introduction, let us relate a couple of items from
Advertising Age that will set the tone for our paper. The
first item [8] is a report of a regional meeting at which the
following product concept was used as a vehicle for creative
discussion: a vitamin enriched decaffinated coffee. We don't
know what to make of such a product and we're not sure anybody
else does either. But, it's not a totally unreasonable notion,
and one of the things that occurs to us is what do people do
with these kinds of concepts? How would such a product be categorized? What does it belong with? How does it get meanings
associated with it?

This process of categorization is fundamental to consumer
behavior. When we categorize we render discriminably different
things equivalent. We group products into classes and respond
to them in terms of their class membership rather than their
uniqueness [3, p. 1; 9, p. 382]. In so doing we simplify our
lives a great deal in terms of our behavior and information
processing. We throw away a lot of information in forming categories and this allows us to respond to many products in terms
of a very few cues or key defining attributes.

Another item we saw was the report of a talk by Mr. Harper
of Needham, Harper & Steers in which he was talking about values and "feather" values. These two catch words were used to
refer respectively to simplification in life styles versus the
self-gratification, enhancement-of-self orientation. This
"earth-feather" distinction appeals to us because it suggests
that at a very high level of abstraction people are making fundamental directional choices. By choosing one path instead of
another you eliminate everything along the non-chosen path from
consideration. By classifying things as "earth" or "feather",
a lot of time and effort is conserved. The direction indicated
at such high levels of generality may not be predictive of
where a person ends up, but they do specify vast areas of
choice where the person won't be found. This is another process of simplification that is useful to consumers and therefore represents a fruitful area of study.

When we say that fundamental directions are indicated at

high levels of generality we join the issue of the relation between values and behavior. Even if the notion that people have
values representing enduring general orientations is accepted
[9], we still have to explain the mechanism by which these basic values govern consumer choice behavior. Our talk this
morning involves a mechanism by which this process may occur.

CONSUMER CATEGORIZATION PROCESSES

Product Classes

Basic to the study of consumer behavior is the concept of
product class. Product class is a set of brands seen as closely suitable for one another in meeting a consumer's needs [6,
p. 279]. Every industry has its notion of product class which
is convenient to either manufacturing or marketing or some aspect of the way the firms in an industry look at their markets.
These conceptions of product class may not represent the way
consumers think about products. Each person's idea of substi-
tutability in meeting a given need may be a bit different.
Consumers are not necessarily complex - but, they certainly are
different. Using complex explanations to account for a multitude of simple idiosyncratic systems may lead us astray in
seeking a true understanding of consumer functioning.

Classes Based on Denotative Meaning

Focusing on class as a concept on its own, apart from that
of product class, leads us into the broader topic of conceptual
systems. A class is a set of objects having a common defining
attribute [3, p. 30]. Classes are the building blocks of conceptual systems. There are various types of conceptual systems
which are pertinent to consumer behavior. A conceptual system
can be based on the denotative meanings of products. Denotative meanings are verbal descriptions or psychophysical refer-
ents [6, p. 34]. As an example, Table 1 shows a taxonomy of
drinks based on their physical properties. The fact that this
is one of many ways to classify drinks is not at issue here.

This classification system makes a fundamental division between drinks as to their alcoholic content. The non-alcoholic
drinks are divided into major types and the soft drinks are further separated into those which are carbonated or non-carbonated. At the lowest level in the system, the non-carbonated
drinks are separated into the major product forms presently on
the market. Not shown is the multitude of brands and flavors
that are subsumed by the general product forms.

Needless to say, there is a tremendous variety of product
choices available to consumers. How consumers group these pro-

TABLE 1

DENOTATIVE

CONCEPTUAL STRUCTURE FOR DRINKS

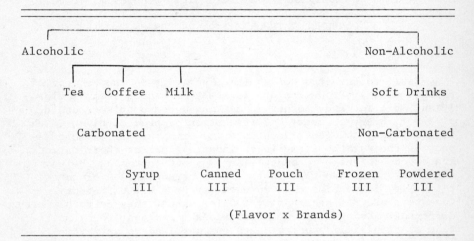

(Flavor x Brands)

ducts is in large measure a function of how they think about
them. When we talk about alcoholic beverages as a class we ignore whether a particular product is champagne or tequila or
beer or wine or scotch or whiskey, or a great variety of other
alternatives and just focus on one defining attribute - alcoholic content. According to one definition of abstraction
level based on inclusiveness, this represents an abstract level
of categorization [10]. It brings together in one class many
many different objects. As such it represents a great simplification in organizing one's attitudes about these products.

Perception and Cognition in Categorization

At the lowest level in Table 1 -- the comparison of the
same flavors of different brands and/or forms -- the issue is
largely perceptual. The question here is, can consumers detect
a difference between products? When two different products are
classified together perceptually, it is because differences between them are not taken into account [1, p. 226]. At the
higher levels in the table the issue is one of cognition. Cognition is a deliberate process in our view. It says we are de-
liberately going to disregard some information for the purpose
of simplifying and forming classes [1, p. 226]. Most conceptual systems are based on cognizing as opposed to being based
on perceptual differences. We can form a single class of "tea"
even though many different teas are put in such a class. The
discriminating tea drinker would most likely have more classes

130

or categories or tea than would the typical American tea drinker.

Classes Based on Connotative Meaning

Another basis upon which a conceptual system can be based is connotative meanings. Connotative meanings are personal in nature and tend to be evluative as opposed to being descriptive [6, p. 34]. The example presented in Table 2 has to do with the implications of crunchiness in cereals. Some people just like crunchy cereal - essentially these people have little or no conceptual system relating to the crunchiness of cereal. Others associate "body" with crunchiness. Some of these people feel that body makes the cereal last longer in your mouth, and, as in chewing gum, the longer it lasts the more the flavor experience.

TABLE 2

CONNOTATIVE

CONCEPTUAL STRUCTURE FOR CEREALS

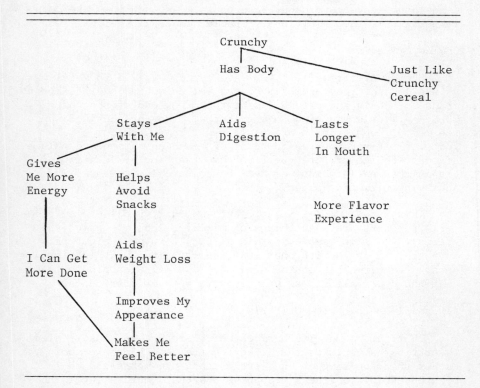

131

Means-Ends Chains

The means-end chain is a concept that brings together values important to the consumer with connotative and denotative meanings and ties these to attributes actually in the products. While there are several different conceptions of means-end chains the one proposed by Howard [5, p. 89] will serve our purposes here. It has the following form:

$$\text{terminal values} \rightarrow \text{instrumental values} \rightarrow \text{choice criteria} \rightarrow \text{product attributes}$$

Terminal and instrumental values are defined within the context of Rokeach's theory of values [9]. Terminal values are defined as end states of existence toward which people strive (e.g., comfortable life, world at peace, happiness, pleasure, wisdom, etc.). Instrumental values are defined to be more closely tied to "doing" than to "being" as are terminal values. In terms of the means-end chain, terminal values represent the goals toward which we strive and instrumental values define the means by which we approach those goals. As such they are more like traits (e.g., ambitious, capable, cheerful, helpful, etc.).

Choice Criteria

Choice criteria [5, p. 28] are conceptualized as serving values in that they mediate between values on one end of the means-end chain and attributes at the other end of the chain. Choice criteria are tied to attributes. They are defined as the mental counterparts of attributes. They grow out of efforts to satisfy motives in terms of reaching out toward valued states. Choice criteria perform this function by identifying brands that satisfy motives and, hence, are instrumental in achieving ultimate values.

This type of model is attribute-based (typical choice criteria for cars are such things as mileage, economy, price and status). In some respects it is difficult to go against this approach; it deals with what is actually being built into products. And, it has been the domain of the miltuiattribute model that has dealt almost exclusively with product attributes.

Alternatives to Choice Criteria

There are some alternatives which are not so closely tied to attributes; this is the direction from which we are coming. Rather than focusing on one level within the means-end chain, we are seeking to find a mechanism that cuts across levels to

132

mediate between connotative meanings at the values level to denotative meanings at the attribute level. This suggests an approach that is biased toward uncovering what is "in people's heads" as opposed to dealing with what is "in products." If consumers are buying "hope" or "sizzle" in terms of benefits, they are buying something different from, although implied by, attributes. We feel that introducing a mechanism that is oriented toward this view will open up this area to more individually based models which permit greater understanding of the consumer.

DISTINCTIONS

Definition

Our solution to the means-end chain problem of specifying a mechanism by which the links in the chain are held together lies in a concept called a distinction. A distinction is a lot like a Kellyian construct - it is a way in which things are the same and different from other things [7]. It's a class concept - a way of forming related sets of classes. It is definitely an either/or concept. Its dichotomous nature says that a distinction is a filter that is in the person which is imposed upon events by classing them as either this or that.

Examples

Some examples will make the concept clearer. In the domain of television a distinction many viewers seem to make is between programs that are "entertaining" and those that "make me think." "Makes me think" or "entertaining" is a distinction many viewers find useful in identifying programs they won't watch. The recent mini-series, King, shown on NBC might have fallen into this category. If entertainment values are dominated by presentation of material that challenges the viewer's thinking processes the results are usually not too good for the Nielsen ratings.

Another example can be drawn from the area of nutrition and diet: "fattening" or "healthful" (or "not fattening" or "thinning"). The nature of a distinction lies in the relation between the two classes formed by the application of the distinction. If "healthful" represents the other pole, the nature of the distinction lies in suggesting that foods which are fattening are not good for you. If "not fattening" is the opposite pole to "fattening," the distinction may be aiding the person in identifying foods to avoid so as to not gain weight. If "thinning" is the opposite pole, the holder of the distinction may be seeking foods to actively aid in losing weight. In this battle the person may identify a food as either a weight-gainer or weight loser.

Logical Negation

The "not fattening" alternative deserves some special mention. The use of logical negation ("not") to form alternative poles in distinctions results in the formation of single classes. There is no common property holding the "not" category together. The only thing "not fattening" foods have in common is that they are not fattening. In other words, a single class of fattening foods is formed and everything else is put in an "other" category. This single class alternative is very useful to consumers and represents the minimum necessary structure for building a conceptual system.

Using Distinctions to Classify Events

Another example of a distinction, and, one which has a slightly different orientation, is exemplified by "stressful or healthful." One of the methods in helping people to stop smoking is to get them to identify circumstances which trigger smoking behavior. If stress is the key, the person would be asked to identify stressful situations in his daily life. Such situations could cover a variety of activities from arguments and business meetings, to missing traffic lights. If the person can be taught to treat these events as a single class of "stressful" situations he can react to them as a class. In this case the distinction "stressful or healthful" helps in providing a category into which events can be put. Having classified an event as stressful or healthful, appropriate responses can be learned based on the key defining properties of the distinction.

Hierarchical Structures

A last example deals with growth and change in distinctions. Most all persons have a "male or female" distinction. Such a distinction is fairly basic - and, it's usually fairly easy to apply to people. Many people are also likely to have a "masculine or feminine" distinction. Such a distinction may be subordinate to the male-female distinction; that is, people may first classify a person as male or female, and then based on life style, appearance, or certain behaviors, classify this male or female as masculine or feminine. In effect, the person has two "masculine-feminine" distinctions.

MALE   FEMALE
                          or
Masculine or Feminine   Masculine or Feminine

134

Through cultural change, the unisex movement, emotional growth, radicalism or whatever, the person may change to where he has a superordinate masculine-feminine distinction that cuts across sex. Behaviors are examined as to whether they are masculine or feminine before the sex of the person is taken into account. It can be said that there has been some growth in that the masculine-feminine distinction has evolved to a higher order of abstraction.

MASCULINE   FEMININE

or

Male or Female   Male or Female

PURPOSE

The specific purpose of this study if to show how consumers group products at different levels of abstraction. Consumers tend to be concrete - to operate at the lowest cognitive level. If we want to get truly meaningful results we may have to push them up the ladder of abstraction to get responses which are closer to the values that govern behavior. Not all behavior is a function of values. But systematic behavior other than habit and simple preference may be tied to the values hierarchy.

In terms of the specific parameters of the study we want to examine the number of categories consumers use in grouping products at different levels of abstraction. The hypothesis is that fewer categories will be used as the distinctions become broader and less concrete. We also want to examine the nature of the distinctions used at different levels of abstraction. We suspect that they would move from physical characteristics of products upward to benefits and functions, and finally to values at the highest level.

METHODOLOGY

The methodology associated with this study has three parts. First, the distinctions have to be generated; second, the higher level distinctions have to be elicited from respondents based on their initial distinctions; and third, respondents have to sort products into categories based on the distinctions they gave representing their different levels of abstraction.

Eliciting Distinctions

Distinctions were obtained from respondents using a modified Repertory Grid technique [7]. The approach consists of giving respondents five triads (see Table 3). The respondents were instructed to try to think of a way in which all three objects in each triad could be compared. Then respondents were asked to state how two of the drinks differed from the third.

TABLE 3

TRIADS USED IN ELICITING DISTINCTIONS

Triad			
1	Fruit Juice	Milk	Fruit Drink
2	Soft Drink	Fruit Drink	Fruit Juice
3	Milk	Water	Beer
4	Coffee	Fruit Juice	Water
5	Beer	Soft Drink	Fruit Drink

Generic product names were used to increase the generalizability of the distinctions. We didn't want to get distinctions which applied only to three drinks in any particular triad. Respondents were asked to compare the three drinks before giving distinctions to force them out of the easy choices such as "two are fruit and one is milk." By forcing people to relate all three drinks as a set we were trying to get our respondents to think dimensionally (drinks have to be the same in some way to be different - if not, they are simply not comparable.)

The product class used for studying distinctions and their application to products was "drinks." Drinks were chosen because it was felt that people would be familiar with all the types and brands used in the study.

The data were gathered in a mall setting. A research company was used which has a store-front location in a large mall in Southern California. Their regular interviewers were used (we did have an all-morning training session). The most difficult part of the study for the interviewers was the freedom they had within the context of the protocol to interact with the respondents in developing rapport and probing in connection with getting the higher-level distinctions.

Subjects were housewives between the ages of 20 and 49. Fifty-five respondents were intercepted in the mall and asked to come to the research location to participate in a study concerning their attitudes about different types of drinks. (Eight respondents had to be eliminated because of incomplete data.)

After going through some instructions and examples, respondents were given the triads. The interviewer presented each triad and recorded the response before proceeding to the next. Not all respondents were able to provide distinctions for each of the triads.

Laddering - Getting Higher Order Distinctions

The laddering procedure is slightly different from typical field research procedure (although it does have some parallels) [13]. The approach used is based on a procedure developed by Hinkle [4] which was also briefly illustrated in Bannister [2, p. 56]. After the distinctions were elicited from respondents, the interviewer went back through the distinctions one at a time. Respondents were asked which pole of their distinctions they preferred. (Do you prefer drinks which are _____ or _____ ?). Then they were asked why they preferred drinks that were _____ (interviewers filled in the preferred pole). The answer to the Why? question yielded a second-level distinction which became the basis for generating a third-level distinction repeating the same procedure. The procedure was repeated until the respondent could no longer answer the Why? question.

Sorting Products on the Basis of Distinctions

The longest chain of distinctions obtained from the laddering procedure was used as the basis upon which the respondents were to sort the products. Twenty-three drinks (see Table 4) were used as stimuli. Each drink name was printed upon a small slip of paper. The slips were given to the respondent to look through. The two poles of the first-level distinction were written on two index cards and put in front of the respondent. The respondents were told they were to sort the products into categories such that products which were similar on the basis indicated by the distinction would be put in the same categories. They were told they could use between 2 categories and 23 categories. After the respondents sorted the drinks the results were recorded and the respondents were given the second-level distinctions as the basis for re-sorting the drinks. This process was repeated for each of the distinctions in the chosen chain.

RESULTS

Relative Number of Categories Used

One of the things we were interested in was whether respondents would use fewer categories in sorts at higher levels of abstraction than in sorts based on initial, lower-level dis-

TABLE 4

DRINKS USED IN SORTING TASK

(A) Fresh Orange Juice
(B) Hi-C Orange Drink
(C) Coca-Cola
(D) Hawaiian Punch
(E) Regular Whole Milk
(F) Tap Water
(G) Bottled Water
(H) Wyler's Lemonade
(I) Lowenbrau Beer
(J) Yuban Regular Coffee
(K) Welch's Grape Juice
(L) Tang
(M) 7-Up
(N) Gatorade
(O) Non-Fat Milk
(P) Oceanspray Cranberry Juice
(Q) Dr. Pepper
(R) Welchade Grape Drink
(S) Brim Decaffinated Coffee
(T) Pabst Beer
(U) Treesweet Canned Orange Juice
(V) Diet Pepsi
(W) Miller's Lite Beer

tinctions. Table 5 shows the relative number of categories used by respondents. Column 1 of this table shows that 40% of the respondents used fewer categories in their third-level sorts as compared to their first-level sorts. However, 23% of the respondents used more categories in their first-level sort than their third-level sort.

However, when those respondents who could only supply three levels in their distinction chains are separated from the rest of the respondents (see column 2) it can be seen that 36% of them used more categories and 64% used the same number of categories in their last sort as compared to their first-level sort.

Column 3 of Table 5 shows the third-level sort for those respondents whose chains had more than three levels. Their pattern is completely different from those respondents who could only supply a chain with three levels of distinctions in it. Fifty-six percent of these respondents used fewer categories and only 18% used more categories in their third-level sorts as com-

138

TABLE 5

RELATIVE NUMBER OF CATEGORIES BY LEVEL OF SORT

Relative Number of Categories	Level-3 Compared to Level-1			Highest Level Compared to Level-1 for Respondents with More Than 3-Levels in Their Chains
	All Respondents	Respondents with Only 3-Levels in Their Chains	Respondents with More Than 3-Levels in Their Chains	
	(47)	(13)	(34)	(34)
Fewer	40%	--	56%	53%
More	23	36%	18	9
Same	37	64	26	38

139

pared to their first-level sorts.

The last column in Table 5 shows the difference in categories used in the last sort compared to the first-level sort
for those respondents who had more than three levels in their
distinction chains. Here, 53% used fewer categories and only
9% used more categories. This finding combined with those for
the other columns in the table suggest that respondents have a
differential ability for abstraction. Those respondents with
longer chains seem better able to cope with the task than do
those who are more concrete.

Number of Categories by Level of Sort

The average number of categories used by respondents shows
a trend in the predicted direction although it is rather flat
(see Table 6). There is a drop from level 1 to level 2. The
average number of categories used then stays rather flat until
the drop at level 6.

TABLE 6

AVERAGE NUMBER OF CATEGORIES BY LEVEL OF SORT

			Level of Sort			
	1	2	3	4	5	6
	(47)	(47)	(47)	(21)	(8)	(5)
Average Number of Categories	3.9	3.4	3.3	3.1	3.1	2.67

Content of Distinction by Level

Table 7 shows a coding a content analysis of the distinctions for each of the first four levels of distinctions. It
can readily be seen that the distinctions at level one were
primarily concerned with contents or physical aspects of the
drinks (e.g., carbonated, alcohol, fruit, sugar, chemicals,
caffeine, etc.). At the second level, functions of the drinks
represent 50% of the distinctions (e.g., nutritious, healthy,
fattening, good for me, weight control, keeps me going, etc.).
The pattern is fairly clear -- initial response is to focus on
physical properties of the drinks -- a concrete approach. When
pushed abit respondents answer the Why? question in terms of
some product function or benefit. At the second leve some res-

140

pondents reply that they simply like the taste, it's refreshing, or some other general preference-type remark.

TABLE 7

CONTENT ANALYSIS OF DISTINCTIONS BY LEVEL OF SORT

| | Level of Sort | | | |
| | 1 | 2 | 3 | 4 |
	(47)	(47)	(47)	(34)
Contents	75%	22%	20%	21%
Function	22	50	50	54
Taste/Preference	3	22	12	7
States	–	5	18	18

The pattern at the third and fourth levels is the same; function-type distinctions dominate. However, a new category of response rises to equal frequency with contents-type distinctions. This category, "states," refers to end-states of the person - it makes me feel good, happy, relaxed, etc. This may be a way the respondent has of saying, "I don't know why" or it may represent the end-state toward which they are striving. In this context the drink is instrumental in helping them achieve that end-state via the other links in the chain of distinctions they have provided.

An Example of Laddering

As each respondent's distinction chain is unique, an example would appear to be a good way of presenting an overall view of their nature. One respondent gave us a "fresh or processed" distinction (see Table 8). When asked which type of drink she preferred she said she like "fresh" best. In response to the Why? question, her distinction was "more vitamins vs. less vitamins." The next level showed a redirection in the chain in that she moved to a "high sugar-low sugar" distinction. The implication here was that drinks high in vitamins were low in sugar (some respondents had a "vitamins-sugar" distinction). From sugar, she moved to calories and then to a function or benefit (weight control). It was from here a key benefit arose in the form of the "size of clothes" distinction. And lastly, the final level was the continued attraction of her husband.

141

It may not be difficult for the reader to appreciate this respondent organizing foods and activities along this critical distinction (keeps my husband at home or out).

TABLE 8

EXAMPLES OF LADDERING

Level	Distinction
1	Fresh or Processed
2	More Vitamins or Less Vitamins
3	Lower Sugar or Higher Sugar
4	Low Calories or High Calories
5	Good for Weight Control or Not Good for Weight Control
6	Smaller Size Clothes or Larger Size Clothes
7	Husband at Home or Husband Out

Category Size in Sorting

Another way of talking about how many categories a person uses is to look at the diversity of things put into the same category. Table 9 shows the results of one person's sort on a "natural-manufactured" distinction. Six categories were used in grouping the 23 drinks. The "most natural" category contains fresh orange juice, both types of milk, both types of water, and grape juice. The next category to the right has regular coffee (notice that Brim, a decaffinated coffee, is more toward the "manufactured" end of the distribution). On the "manufactured" side, the soft drinks were seen as the most manufactured followed by the fruit drinks. The categories used by this respondent were fairly narrow. In capturing what she thought was the essence of her "natural-manufactured" distinction she maintained several levels or degrees of "naturalness" or of "manufacturedness."

Figure 1 shows another person's sorts for three distinctions in her chain. Notice first that she has only used two categories for her "natural-manufactured" distinction. There is high overlap in the drinks considered most natural by this respondent and the previous one (see Table 9). The difference between the two respondents is that the previous subject used 5

142

TABLE 9

A RESPONDENT'S SORTING OF DRINKS INTO 6 CATEGORIES BASED ON A "NATURAL–MANUFACTURED" DISTINCTION

Natural					Manufactured	
Fresh Orange Juice	Regular Coffee	Pabst	Tang	Hi-C	Coca-Cola
Regular Milk	Oceanspray Cranberry Juice	Lowenbrau	Brim Decaffinated Coffee	Hawaiian Punch	7-Up
Tap Water		Millers			Dr. Pepper
Bottled Water	Treesweet Canned Orange Juice			Wyler's Lemonade	Diet Pepsi
Welch's Grape Juice				Gatorade	
Non-Fat Milk				Welch's Grape Drink	

FIGURE 1

A RESPONDENT'S SORTING FOR 23 DRINKS USING 3 DISTRIBUTIONS

	Natural			Manufactured		
	High	Medium	Low	High	Medium	Low
NO CHEMICALS	Fresh Orange Juice		Yuban Coffee	Treesweet Canned Orange Juice	7-Up	Brim Decaffinated Coffee
	Oceanspray Cranberry Juice			Hi-C		
	Regular Milk			Tap Water		
	Bottled Water			Wyler's Lemonade		
	Welch's Grape Juice			Tang		
	Non-Fat Milk			Welch's Grape Drink		
CHEMICALS					Coca-Cola Pabst	
					Dr. Pepper Millers	
					Diet Pepsi Lowenbrau	
					Gatorade	

categories creating homogeneous groups of drinks whereas this respondent used only one group. Evidently, if it wasn't completely natural, it was manufactured.

Also shown in Figure 1, are the arrays for the other two distinctions. She used three categories for "healthy" - "not healthy." Notice here, that manufactured drinks can be high in health, too. And, of course, those drinks containing chemicals are manufactured.

Perceptual Maps Based on Category Groupings

The final part of our analysis of these data was to develop a perceptual map so as to illustrate the spatial relations between the drinks at different levels of abstraction. Following a procedure of Rosenberg and Kim [11] a matrix of distances between drinks was calculated. The measure of distance is based on the number of times across people that two drinks are put in the same category. The more frequently two drinks are put in the same category the more similar they are; two drinks not put in the same category by most respondents would be far apart. Three such distance matrices were calculated for the first, third, and fifth-level sorts. Each sort's matrix was submitted separately to POLYCON [12], a multidimensional scaling program. The fit of the derived distances to the original distances was good for all three matrices (Kendal stress values of .093, .093, and .076 respectively).

Figure 2 shows the product space for level 1. The axes are labeled on the basis of the known properties of the drinks. There are two clusters of healthy drinks which are close together and removed from other drinks. The fruit drinks (as opposed to the juices) are tightly clustered together. At this level, the soft drinks are removed from the fruit drinks indicating that few people in their first-level sorts put the fruit drinks and the soft drinks in the same category.

Figure 3 shows the product space for the level 3 sorts. At this higher level of abstraction, all the waters, milks, and juices form a single cluster in the healthy-natural quadrant. The fruit drinks are slightly more dispersed as compared to the level 1 space. There is a slight tendency for Hi-C, Gatorade, and Tang to pull toward the juices while Hawaiian Punch and Wyler's Lemonade pull down toward the soft drinks.

The level 5 product space is shown in Figure 4. The two milks, the two waters, and orange juice form a tight grouping far removed from other drinks. Ocean Spray Cranberry Juice is by itself, although it is closer to the fruit drinks. Actually, the drinks form a crescent with Welch's Grape Juice the

FIGURE 2

PRODUCT SPACE IN 2-DIMENSIONS BASED ON 1ST-LEVEL DISTINCTIONS*

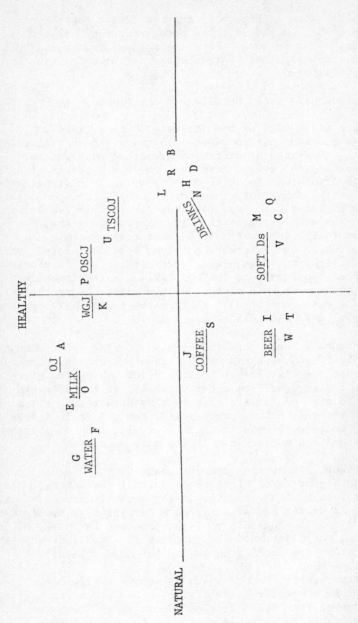

* See Table 4 for key

146

FIGURE 3

PRODUCT SPACE IN 2-DIMENSIONS BASED ON 3RD-LEVEL DISTINCTIONS*

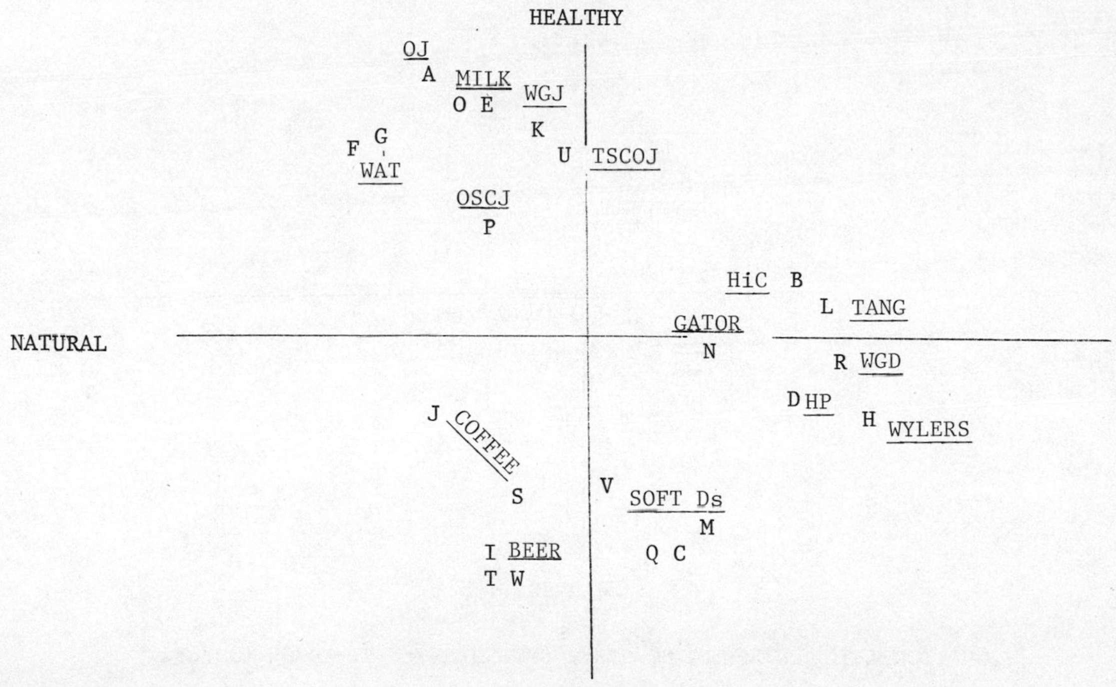

* See Table 4 for key

FIGURE 4

PRODUCT SPACE IN 2-DIMENSIONS BASED ON 5TH-LEVEL DISTINCTIONS*

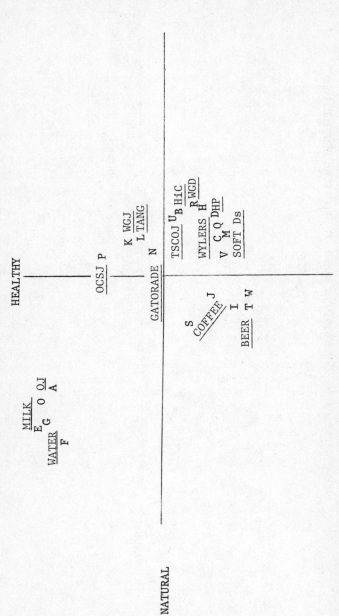

148

*See Table 4 for key

closest to cranberry juice. Tang, Gatorade, canned orange
juice, and Hi-C are at the top of the crescent. At the bottom
of the crescent are the soft drinks which have joined the fruit
drinks at this high level of abstraction. Hawaiian Punch and
Wyler's Lemonade are quite close to the soft drinks. Beer and
coffee are each off by themselves are they were for the other
levels. They share no properties with the other drinks and as
such are not grouped together with them.

DISCUSSION

This research has presented findings which suggest that
the nature of the distinctions consumers make represent useful
information to researchers in their quest to better understand
how consumers structure their words. Our results also point up
the fact that the path of least resistance consumers follow in
responding to our questions may not represent the true basis
upon which they base their decisions. Consumers tend to be
concrete in their thinking; their groupings of products into
classes reflects this orientation. Products are narrowly con-
strued on the basis of physical similarities.

When consumers are pushed up their ladders of abstraction
they are forced to become more abstract in the way they think
about products and the interactions of products with their
lives. As consumers' levels of abstraction are raised, the implications of physical product characteristics for benefits,
and in turn, of benefits for values become apparent. Developing an understanding of these means-end hierarchies should aid
researchers in learning to see the world as consumers see it.

Consumers are not tidy and neat in that their conceptual
systems are full of inconsistencies and lack integration.
Overly rational approaches emphasizing low levels of abstraction (the attribute level) are not the path to understanding.
Methods must be found which allow the consumer to choose his
own basis for structuring his world. We hope distinctions ful-
fill this role and that the insight they provide will be of use
in helping us to ask better questions.

REFERENCES

1. Anderson, B.F. Cognitive Psychology. New York: Academic
    Press, 1975.

2. Bannister, D. "Science Through the Looking Glass," in D.
    Bannister, ed., Perspectives in Personal Construct Theory.
    London: Academic Press, 1970, pp. 47-62.

3. Bruner, J.S., J. Goodnow, and G.A. Austin. A Study of

Thinking. New York: John Wiley & SOns, Inc., 1956.

4. Hinkle, D. The Change of Personal Constructs from the
    Viewpoint of a Theory of Construct Implication. Unpub-
    lished Doctoral Dissertation, Ohio State University, Col-
    umbus, Ohio, 1965.

5. Howard, J.A. Consumer Behavior: Application of Theory.
    New York: McGraw Hill Book Company, 1977.

6. Howard, J.A. and Sheth, J.N. The Theory of Buyer Behavior.
    New York: John Wiley and Sons, Inc., 1969.

7. Kelly, G.A. The Psychology of Personal Constructs. New
    York: Norton, 2 Volumes, 1955.

8. O'Connor, J.J., "Coffee Gets Creative Juice Flowing," Ad-
    vertising Age, March 6, 1978.

9. Rokeach, M., The Nature of Human Values. New York: Free
    Press, 1973.

10. Rosch, E., C.B. Mervis, W.D. Gray, D.M. Johnson, and P.
     Boyes-Braem, "Basic Objects in Natural Categories," Cog-
     nitive Psychology, 8 (1976), pp. 382-439.

11. Rosenberg, S. and M.P. Kim, "The Method of Sorting as a
     Data-Gathering Procedure in Multivariate Research," Multi-
     variate Behavioral Research, 10 (October, 1975), pp. 489-
     502.

12. Young, F.W. POLYCON Users Manual. A FORTRAN-IV Program
     for Polynomial Conjoint Analysis. Chapel Hill, North
     Carolina: L.L. Thurstone Psychometric Laboratory Report
     No. 104, 1972.

13. Young, S. and Feigin, B., "Using the Benefit Chain for Im-
     proved Strategy Formulation," Journal of Marketing, 39
     (1975), pp. 72-74.

ARE ATTITUDE MODELS APPROPRIATE FOR MASS TV ADVERTISING?

John L. Lastovicka
Temple University

Beginning with Andreasen [2], consumer behaviorists have looked primarily to attitude theory to explain brand choice behavior. This orientation is reflected in the attitude concept's central role in the comprehensive models of consumer behavior [9, 12]. This preoccupation with attitude is due to the belief that attitudes are an antecedent condition of behavior. For example, Myers and Reynolds [27, p. 146] claim: "In a broad sense, purchase decisions are based almost solely upon attitudes existing at the time of purchase, however these attitudes might have formed."

Consequently, marketing management has direct interest in understanding the process of attitude change. Runyon [35, p. 282] observes: "It is generally recognized among marketing practitioners that attitude change is the primary goal of marketing strategy. Product design, service, price, packaging, and promotional activity are the basic tools available to the marketing manager for changing consumer attitudes." The multiattribute attitude models of Fishbein [10] and Rosenberg [33] have provided a general framework for promotional strategies aimed at changing brand attitudes. For example, these multiattribute models can suggest to an advertising manager how he ought to attempt to change consumer perceptions about his brand in order to favorably influence attitudes and behavior.

In the hundreds of consumer behavior studies that have grappled with the theoretical problems in the multiattribute models, as well as the pragmatic papers which suggest advertising based on these models [7,6], no one has questioned if attitude is really an appropriate concept with relevance to most consumer goods and services. It has only been recently that Kassarjian [14,15] has seriously raised this question. Kassarjian suggests that one reason for the lack of explained variance and the many unresolved theoretical issues in consumer behavior attitude studies may be the difference in focal points between social psychology, the discipline of origin for attitude theory, and consumer behavior. Whereas social psychologists deal with important and emotional topics like racism and politics, consumer behaviorists primarily work with objects like laundry detergents, canned peas and toothpaste, which may have less involvement for the consumer. Although goods like stereo components and automobiles can be as involving for some

consumers as the topics in the original social psychology attitude studies, it can be argued that the attitude concept may be
entirely inappropriate for many low involvement product classes. Following Lastovicka and Gardner [24], a low involvement
product class is one in which the consumer perceives little
linkage to important values and is a product class where there
is little commitment to any of the brands.

The suggestion that buyers are not highly involved with
most consumer products can put advertising management at a
loss. Most of the theory advertising message management know-
ingly draws from is attitude theory; yet the bulk of advertising TV dollars are spent on low-involvement product classes
[34]. Thus, the theoretical basis on which much of advertising
message planning is predicated may not be appropriate for much
of mass TV advertising.

DO CONSUMERS REALLY HAVE ATTITUDES TOWARDS BRANDS?

Before discussing the relevance of attitude to low involvement consumers products, it is necessary to deal with the
problem of defining attitude. If a concept's relevance is to
be evaluated, then there ought to be agreement as to what the
concept represents. One widely quoted definition of attitude
is by Krech, Crutchfield and Ballachey [17] who consider attitude to be: "enduring systems of positive or negative evaluations, emotional feelings and pro and con action tendencies
with respect to social objects." This is consistent with Thurstone's [42] classic position that attitude is simply the
amount of affect for or against some object. Essentially an attitude represents a person's enduring favorable or unfavorable
global evaluation about some object. Attitudes are reflected
in statements such as: "I like Pintos!" or "Vegas are lemons!"
Although attitudes may have implicit action tendencies, attitudes do not represent the knowledge that a person has about a
given object nor do attitudes represent a person's observed behavior towards a given object.

Arguments suggesting that consumers do not have attitudes
towards brands in low involvement product classes can be found
in three areas: functional theories of attitude, concept formation, and low involvement theory itself. Each argument will be
discussed.

Functional Theory

A clue for understanding why a person may or may not have
an attitude, or an enduring affective global evaluation about
some object, can be obtained from the functional attitude theories [16, 39]. As will become apparent, by paying attention to

152

what an attitude does for its holder, the idea that consumers have attitudes for all brands considered or purchased becomes questionable. The five functions of attitude discussed below are taken from Lutz's [25] review and synthesis of the functional attitude theories.

The first basic need that an attitude may satisfy is "value expression." For example, a teenager may hold and express favorable attitudes towards rock music to clearly establish status as an independent teenager who is not under parental domination. Such an attitude is used to help express an individual's values and self-concept. This function, or reason for holding an attitude, seems inoperable for low involvement product classes. For example, it is highly unlikely that many consumers would hold an enduring like towards a brand of tuna fish or bread in order to express self-concept. By definition low involvement products have little linkage to values. Consequently, this first function seems inapplicable.

The second function that attitudes perform is "ego-defense." Prejudicial attitudes are an often given example of this function. A hatred for one racial group may help the holder of such an attitude think less of his own shortcomings and consequently more of himself. Such attitudes, which protect individuals from both internal and external threats, seem to have little place in the world of low involvement products. Very little of the ego, if anything, would seem to be protected with a like or dislike for Star Kist tuna or any other low involvement product.

The third function, the "satisfaction of social needs" function, recognizes that holding and expressing certain attitudes can help an individual become accepted by certain social groups. For example, a new hourly wage employee may have to express certain negative attitudes about management to be accepted by his new co-workers. Again it is highly unlikely that acceptance by most social groups would be aided by expressing like or dislike about unimportant consumer brands.

The fourth function, the "utilitarian" function, recognizes that people have attitudes to summarize past or present beliefs about the want satisfaction of different objects. An attitude held on a utilitarian basis helps the holder maximize reward and minimize punishment. The multiattribute attitude model seems to fit this function exactly. However, when it is pointed out that consumers perceive little -- if any -- distinction between brands along want satisfying dimensions in low involvement product classes [29], the notion of an affective summary becomes meaningless. Why have utilitarian attitudes about different brands that are basically all alike? If an

153

identical amount of need satisfaction is perceived in any brand in a product class, then it makes little sense to have utilitarian based attitudes for each brand.

The fifth and final function served by attitude is the "knowledge" function. Attitudes serve a need for knowledge according to functional theory, by helping an individual organize his perceptions of the environment and provide clarity for his personal view of the world. It would appear to be far simpler for the consumer to organize perceptions of the little differences between brands in low involvement product classes with beliefs and not attitudes. Krugman [18] claims that consumers use trivial knowledge about brands picked up from television advertising. Krugman's theory does not suggest that attitude, or affect, is learned from the mass media. For example, the consumer's need to organize the world of toilet paper brands would seem to be most easily accomplished with a set of very basic descriptive beliefs like: "This brand is sold by that grocer on TV" and "This other brand is supposed to be soft as a cloud," rather than a set of attitudes.

On the face of it, attitudes for low involvement products seem functionless. According to functional theory, in order to have an attitude for a given object, the object must be related to conception of self, or be linked to important values, or be of importance to some social group, or have perceived differential need satisfaction from other objects. For the bulk of products with heavy mass TV advertising, none of the above functional qualities seem to be met.

CONCEPT FORMATION

Support for the notion that consumers do not necessarily have attitudes towards brands is also found in the theoretical positions of those advocating a concept-formation approach to attitude acquisition. Rhine [32], for example, argues that all social objects can have associated with them two types of mediating responses. As shown in Figure 1, a stimulus object can elicit two internal responses from a subject. One of these responses represents the identification or categorization of the social object. This descriptive labeling response is shown as r_d in Figure 1. The other response is the evaluative or affective attitudinal response labeled r_e. Rhine's position is that the evaluative responses are not as basic as the descriptive responses. He argues that although people may have acquired denotative meaning about an object, they do not necessarily have connotative meanings. Osgood et al [28] and Fishbein [10] have a similar, but different position. They argue that there is always an evaluative response for every object, but they point out that in the case of unfamiliar or novel stimuli the evaluative response may be neutral.

FIGURE 1

A STIMULUS OBJECT ELICITING TWO RESPONSES

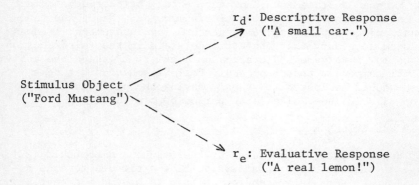

r_d: Descriptive Response ("A small car.")

Stimulus Object ("Ford Mustang")

r_e: Evaluative Response ("A real lemon!")

This writer argues that neutral attitudes, rather than being ambivalent tendencies resulting from the presence of many favorable and unfavorable components, are indifference tendencies which represent very few components. A scaling study reported by Lastovicka and Gardner [23] shows low involved respondents have fewer dimensions in their cognitive map of automobiles than those higher involved. The absence of a highly differentiated cognitive structure for the low involved would suggest that their "neutral" attitudes are not the result of weighing and counterbalancing the pros and cons of each brand. Rather than ambivalence, a neutral evaluative response for a low involvement object exhibits indifference and the lack of any attitude at all.

Although consumers may learn some denotative meaning about brands, they are not theoretically obliged to love or hate these brands. Just because a consumer knows that Wonder Bread "has spots on the package," this does not oblige the same consumer to carry around an enduring like or dislike for Wonder Bread.

LOW INVOLVEMENT THEORY

A final area of support for the notion that consumers do not necessarily have brand attitudes comes from low involvement theory. Krugman's [18] theory suggests that advertising for low involvement products works in a COGNITIVE → CONATIVE → AFFECTIVE hierarchy of effects. Krugman [19, p. 225] writes:

"In short, with low involvement product choices, we might look for product adoption through gradual shifts in perceptual structure, aided by repetition, activated by behavioral choice situations, and <u>followed at some time</u> by attitude change (italics added)". Ray et al [29] have suggested that attitude change comes very soon after purchase.

Krugman's statements, however, about attitude development are nebulous in regard to the time dimension. Given the functional and concept formation arguments just presented, it does not seem necessary that the attitude stage in the third section of the low involvement hierarchy need exist. Perhaps the attitudinal component that supposedly follows behavior "at some · time" should be looked at as only having the potential to develop at some indefinite later period of time.

EMPIRICAL EVIDENCE

Survey research conducted by Lastovicka and Bonfield [22] suggests that although consumers do have attitudes towards social issues, such as a stand on abortion, consumers do <u>not</u> necessarily have attitudes towards brands in low involvement product classes.

<u>Sample</u>. Using random digit dialing [41], a sample of 105 household numbers from the city of Philadephia was generated during the fall of 1977. Of the 105, 57 agreed to participate in the tape recorded telephone interview, 34 refused and 19 could not be reached despite a series of call backs. After accounting for futher losses due to tape recording – jammed tapes, recording over previous interviews and garbled tapes – 49 useable cases remained. Each of the 49 respondents was a female head of household.

<u>Questions</u>. The goal of the research was to determine if consumers have <u>any</u> attitudes for an array of consumer product brands and social issue stands. Typically, in marketing research, the interest is in measuring direction and magnitude and not presence or absence of attitude. That is, typically a researcher measures whether consumers like or dislike a given object and, furthermore, measures the degree of the liking or disliking. The familiar Likert or semantic differential scales are commonly used to tap direction and magnitude.

In his review of attitude measurement in <u>The Handbook of Social Psychology</u>, Scott [37] suggests only one method, the open questioning method, to measure whether or not there are attitudes. With the open questioning procedure respondents are presented with a question that invites expression of attitude, if any, (or beliefs, arguments for or against, or behavior) about a specific object.

The questioning procedure was identical to Fishbein's elicitation technique in which respondents are asked to give responses to the same stimulus word in a free association situation. (See Ryan and Bonfield [36] for an excellent discussion of the elicitation technique.) The list of specific objects used in the current study is shown in Table 1.

TABLE 1

SOCIAL OBJECTS USED IN THE LASTOVICKA - BONFIELD STUDY

Brands in Different Product Classes:

1. Wonder Bread
2. Pepperidge Farm Bread
3. Sunbeam Bread
4. Crest Toothpaste
5. Ultra-Brite Toothpaste
6. Close-Up Toothpaste
7. Charmin Toilet Paper
8. White Cloud Toilet Paper
9. Cottenelle Toilet Paper
10. AMC Gremlin Automobile
11. Ford Mustang II
12. Chevrolet Vega

Stands on Different Social Issues:

13. The city charter of Philadelphia should be changed to allow a mayor to run for more than two terms in office.
14. The city charter of Philadelphia should not be changed.
15. The pregnant woman should be allowed to make up her own mind as to whether or not she wants an abortion.
16. No abortions should be performed.

An example of the specific question used was: "What comes into your mind when I mention 'Wonder Bread'?" Besides mentioning the specific object this question bends over backwards not to suggest a dimension of response. The question does not suggest attitude - as in "How do you like?" nor belief as in "What do you know about?" - the question used, in and of itself, does not suggest a particular response. Probes were used in the questioning to allow the respondents the opportunity to say as much as they wanted to about each object.

The advantages of the open question technique are twofold. First, it does not suggest particular answers which might be accepted by acquiescent respondents. This was not a situation using a semantic differential where respondents, who might not care at all about the specific attitude objects, report perceptions that they really might not have. Second, it permits the researcher to determine whether or not an attitude is held. As in any research situation tradeoffs exist between advantages and disadvantages. Primarily because of its advantages the open question technique has the disadvantage of being time-consuming to code.

Coding. The responses elicited from the 49 respondents in the tape recorded telephone interviews were coded by three coders. The following response classifications were given operational definitions [21]:

1. descriptive belief
2. evaluative belief
3. normative belief
4. articulate attitude
5. inarticulate attitude
6. behavioral intention
7. behavior
8. advertising imagery
9. advertising replay
10. package or point display
11. personal connections
12. counter arguments
13. source derogation
14. curiosity

Each coder has graduate coursework in consumer behavior and had been trained in the application of these definitions to the coding. Reliability was accessed by having each coder judge a common set of 15 interviews. The intercoder reliability, averaged across all categories for the first thought for each of the 16 objects, was .65.

Findings. Because of space limitations, only a small part of the analysis will be discussed here. Figure 2 shows a frequency distribution for some of the coding of the first responses elicited to four specific objects. This particular four object set includes two consumer brands, "Wonder Bread" and "Charmin" toilet paper, and two stands on social issues, "allowing May Rizzo to change the Philadelphia City Charter in or-

158

der that he may run for third term in office" and "allowing a woman to make up her own mind, without restriction, regarding an abortion." Previous research [13] has found that social issues are in the high involvement realm and consumer products are generally in the low involvement realm. The primary hypothesis was that attitudes should be present for the social issue stands, but not for the brands. Simpler beliefs were expected for the brands.

As Figure 2 demonstrates, the findings are clearly in line with expectations. Philadelphia housewives do not carry around enduring evaluations about brands in their minds. Every type of evaluation -- evaluative belief, nomative belief and articulate attitude -- is virtually absent for the brands. Much simple denotative meaning about these brands is carried around by this sample of housewives. Other analysis shows that the majority of the brand descriptive beliefs are from advertising and packaging verbal replay and imagery. Attitudes and other evaluative beliefs, however, seem to be alive and well with social issues. Two clear-cut patterns seem present between responses to consumer brands and social issue stands.

The conservative measurement approach used here suggests that Philadelphia female head of households do not have attitudes towards everyday consumer brands. For the most part, these women do not have attitudes towards brands in the manner that attitude theorists would suggest. Attitudes seem primarily reserved for important social issues.

WHERE DO WE GO FROM HERE?

The first section of this paper has argued against the appropriateness of the attitude concept for low involvement product classes. In this second section of the paper, theoretical bases for brand choice behavior -- other than attitude theory -- will be discussed. Special attention will be paid to the practical application of these alternative theoretical bases to advertising message planning.

A HIERARCHY OF BEHAVIORAL THEORIES

Marketers and consumer researchers have recently been reminded of other, though less fashionable, theoretical alternatives to the "think before you act" approach of attitude theory [30, 26]. These challenging theoretical alternatives, connectionist and reinforcement theories, argue that behavior is not controlled from within by attitudes - but from outside the consumer. Watson's [43] work on connectionist theory contends that repeated continuity of stimulus and response is all that is necessary for learning. The more sophisticated rein-

159

FIGURE 2

PERCENTAGE OF FIRST THOUGHTS (FOR SELECTED SOCIAL OBJECTS)
THAT FALL INTO CERTAIN CODING CLASSIFICATIONS*

(n = 49)

Charmin Toilet Paper:

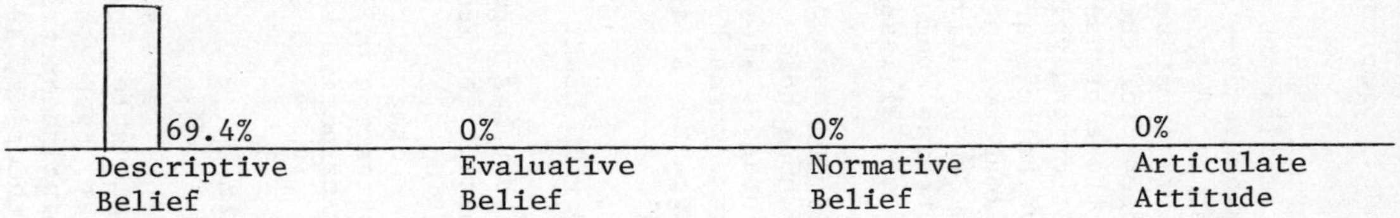

Descriptive Belief	Evaluative Belief	Normative Belief	Articulate Attitude
69.4%	0%	0%	0%

Wonder Bread:

Descriptive Belief	Evaluative Belief	Normative Belief	Articulate Attitude
51.0%	0%	0%	5%

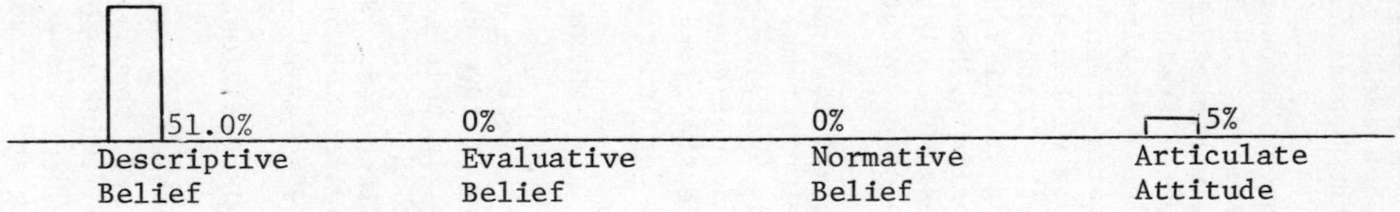

FIGURE 2 (CONTINUED)

Changing the Philadelphia Charter:

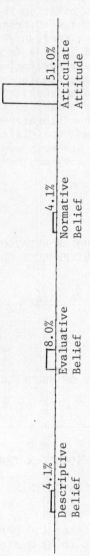

| 4.1% | 8.0% | 4.1% | 51.0% |
| Descriptive Belief | Evaluative Belief | Normative Belief | Articulate Attitude |

The Pro-Abortion Stand:

| 14.3% | 8.2% | 16.3% | 49.10% |
| Descriptive Belief | Evaluative Belief | Normative Belief | Articulate Attitude |

* Coding Classification Definitions:

1. Descriptive Belief: A thought which indicates personal knowledge about the object in terms of denotative meaning. This includes beliefs about the object's relationship to other objects and about characteristics of the object.

2. Evaluative Belief: Statements which indicate that the object will clearly lead to or block a valued goal.

3. Normative Belief: Beliefs about what ought to be done with respect to the object.

4. Articulate Attitude: An overall evaluation about the object.

161

forcement or behavioral modification approach, represented by Skinner's [38] work, centers on reward.

It is proposed that the rational-cognitive decision approach of traditional attitude theory is most appropriate for high involvement products. More precisely, an attitude theory approach is appropriate when the consumer is behaving in a high involvement, active mode. No doubt the purchase of frozen orange juice <u>can</u> be an extensive, intellectualized, high-brain process; but typically such a purchase would be made in a passive manner in line with the consumers' likely perception of this product as trivial. The less structured, simpler connectionist and reinforcement theories seem more appropriate for low involvement products. Figure 3 presents this idea in a pcitorial manner. The essential point in the "hierarchy of theories" is that different theories, or ways of explaining behavior, have their own realms in which they are most appropriate. Depending on the situation, a given theory may best characterize choice behavior.

FIGURE 3

A "HIERARCHY OF THEORIES" APPROACH TO CHOICE BEHAVIOR:
DIFFERENT BEHAVIORAL THEORIES FOR DIFFERENT PRODUCT CLASSES

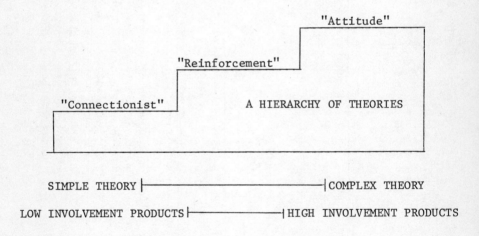

Besides involvement, individual differences and perceptions can also suggest when certain theories ought to be appropriate. A child, for example, because of limitations in cognitive development may only be able to operate, at most, at a reinforcement level. On the other hand, an academic consumer researcher may intellectualize each and every purchase decision made -- regardless of how trivial -- and might consistently operate as expectancy-value attitude models suggest.

Besides face validity, several positions from disciplines other than marketing support the "hierarchies of theories" approach. First and foremost, the work of evolutionary psychologist Gregory Razran [31] should be noted. In his review and synthesis of American behaviorism, Russian Pavlovianism and Western "cognitionism," Razran brings to light the parallel between the complexity of learning behavior and an organism's stage in evolutionary biology. His concern is not with the evolutionary differences in physiology, but rather the systematic development of the mind. In tracing learning from the simple habituation of protozoa to the symbolic learning of primates, Razran proposes that the mind of man is a hierarchy of ascending levels of learning. Razran's [31, p. 290] central thesis is:

> . . . the psychology and underlying neurophysiology
> of the human organism is composed of several hier-
> archial processes, (the human mind) is indeed a
> hierarchy of hierarchies. While man is not a dog,
> a pigeon, or a fish -- still dog, pigeon, fish, and
> even sponge mechanisms are within us."

The point is, simple connectionist psychology is not only appropriate for the laboratory rat; such a less structured law of behavior is a good starting point for understanding low involvement consumer behavior as well.

Second, basic brain hemisphere research also supports this "hierarchy of theories." In a recent discussion of low involvement theory, Krugman [20] refers to some basic psychophysiological research [40] which suggests the active decoding of print media, along with speaking, is primarily a left brain hemisphere function; and the passive perception of images, and the viewing of television, is largely a right brain function. Not only do different levels of the mind operate on an independent basis; but the functions associated with the different levels of the mind, active cognition versus passive recognition, have their own neurological locations.

Third, basic work in verbal learning has discussed levels of information processing.[8]. The idea of a hierarchy of processing stages is often referred to as "depth of processing" where greater depth implies a greater degree of semantic or c cognitive analysis. The implication is that meaningful, more involving stimuli will be processed at deeper levels.

Fourth, closer to home, evidence from marketing suggests

that the simpler connectionist approach is the basis for low involvement consumer behavior. The success of stochastic modeling [3] in low involvement product classes, can be interpreted
as being due in part to the contiguity-connectionist position,
the basis of the stochastic models. The input into these models, the prior brand purchase history, are just so many repeated contiguities of brand and purchase.

On the other side of the coin, marketing studies show that
the most appropriate use of attitude theory is in the high involvement realm. In an industrial buying situation [11], a
much stronger relationship between attitude and purchase intention was found with subjects highly involved with truck air
conditioners (r = .55) as opposed to those in a low involvement
group (r = .18). In a consumer setting, similar results were
found [4]. For consumers who thought that non-carbonated grape
drink was of high importance, a strong relationship (r = .75)
held between attitude and intention. For the low involvement
group a weaker relationship (r = .40) was found.

Given the psychological, psychophysiological and marketing
evidence currently available, the primary question seems not to
be whether the "hierarchy of theories" approach to consumer behavior is valid. The primary question seems to be: "For what
products, in what situations and for whom are given levels of
the hierarchy appropriate?" Consumer behavior is only beginning to seek and understand the appropriate boundaries for di-
vergent theories.

The "hierarchy of theories" philosophy provides a link between a product classification system based on involvement and
the consumer's decision process. This approach does not con-
stitute a theory of consumer behavior, but rather a philosophy
-- a set of orientations -- from which applications and research
questions might be drawn. While the large scale models of consumer behavior are useful, it is suggested that they are often
applied outside their proper domains and that more fruitful
questions are generated by the present philosophy.

A SAMPLE APPLICATION: A COPY TYPOLOGY

The advertising copy typology developed in this section
demonstrates how advertising message strategy can be planned
using theoretical bases other than attitude theory. To start,
in designing messages for target audiences who really do not
"give a hoot" about the advertised product, the key to effective
messages does not seem to be in presenting a great deal of information content. In an experimental study [5], ads with high
information content, as opposed to those with low information
content, were found more effective in inducing willingness to

164

buy with high involvement products. With low involvement products, high information content was only marginally more effective. So, it would seem that information-laden comparative advertising is not necessarily best for low involvement products.

A relatively information-barren but frequently observed approach for low involvement copy is the "problem resolution" commercial. Here, in a real life problem presentation, the advocated brand is demonstrated as an excellent solution for the sinus headache or the spilled cup of coffee. In a behavioral modification approach the receiver is vicariously rewarded by the product solution.

Yet many low involvement products are so trivial that it is nearly impossible to capture inherent product drama in the "problem resolution" approach. This real challenge for the copywriter is pointed out by Alderson's inverse law of copy [1, p. 141]: "The more trivial the product the greater the need for an arresting copy theme." When dealing with those most trivial products -- e.g., canned peas, inexpensive ball-point pens or cookies -- a very simple connectionist approach can be an effective base for a copy platform. This approach suggests that increasing familiarity with a brand, simply due to many repeated advertising exposures, increases preferences. Often copy vehicles like Charlie the Tuna or the Keebler Elves are used to create "friendly familiarity" for the brand.

These imaginative copy vehicles provide special benefits for very low involvement products. First, they allow for more enjoyable and entertaining messages. This is a crucial ingredient, for if low involvement advertising depends upon repetition, the advertiser must guard against "overexposure." There appears to be a definite upper limit to the amount of advertising repetition consumers will tolerate. Unless the advertising is smattered with a high degree of entertainment value, this limit may be considerably reduced for a low involvement product's campaign. Second, these copy vehicles provide an easily remembered basis for differentiating one brand from other brands in the same product class. A distinctive creative style may be sufficient in the low involvement situation to create a perceived unique selling proposition. Since there is typically little perceived differentiation in low involvement product classes this is crucial. (Keebler has the Elves, but what do you know about Flavor Kist or Nabisco?)

Rational "reason why" copy, which includes comparative copy, is best used for high involvement products. Such persuasion, based on choice criteria, are appropriately grounded on attitude theory [6,7]. Detailed copy describing the advocated brand on a feature-by-feature basis is infinitely more appropriate for automobiles than for tuna fish.

The essential elements of this copy typology are presented in Figure 4. Within this framework the difference in the three often observed creative approaches seem reconcilable. Implicitly, successful copywriters have an intuitive understanding of the philosophy advocated in this article. The explanation of this practice is the immediate gain of the current copy typology.

FIGURE 4

AN ADVERTISING COPY TYPOLOGY BASED ON AN
INVOLVEMENT DEFINED PRODUCT CLASSIFICATION
SCHEME AND THE "HIERARCHY OF THEORIES" PHILOSOPHY

TYPE OF COPY

		"Problem Resolution or Slice of Life"	"Reason Why"
Theoretical Base	Connectionist	Reinforcement	Attitude
Appropriate Application	Very low involvement products Example: cookies	Low involvement products: Example: over the counter drugs	High involvement products Example: automobiles
Description	Non-product pertinent information Use of a copy vehicle	Problem posed Solution to problem reached with advocated brand Vicarious reinforcement	Product pertinent information based Relies on choice criteria

CONCLUSIONS

This paper suggests that consumers do not necessarily have attitudes for most low involvement products. This observation has two very important implications for planning mass TV advertising for these products.

The first implication is that advertising for low involvement products, perhaps, ought not to be aimed at changing attitudes. This traditional advertising objective should be re-
evaluated. Rather, since consumers do not have attitudes, a
more valid advertising objective might be to create attitudes.

The second implication is that theories other than attitude theory ought to be re-examined for use in message planning.
The copy typology outlined in this paper suggests that learning
theories can have direct use in planning mass TV advertising.
For most low involvement products, an understanding of the
principles of behavior modification, as opposed to the principles of attitude theory, would seem to be a better aid in
planning advertising messages.

REFERENCES

1. Alderson, Wroe. Dynamic Marketing Behavior, A Functional-
   ist Theory of Marketing. Homewood: Irwin, 1965.

2. Andreasen, Alan R. "Attitudes and Customer Behavior: A
   Decision Model," in Lee E. Preston, ed., New Research in
   Marketing. Berkeley: University of California, 1965, 1-16.

3. Bass, Frank M. "The Theory of Stochastic Preference and
   Brand Switching," Journal of Marketing Research 11 (February 1974), 1-20.

4. Bonfield, E.H. "Attitude, Social Influence, Personal Norm,
   and Intention Interactions as Related to Brand Purchase Behavior," Journal of Marketing Research 11 (November 1974),
   379-389.

5. Bowen, Lawrence and Steven H. Chafee. "Product Involvement
   and Pertinent Advertising Appeals," Journalism Quarterly 5
   (Winter 1974), 613-21.

6. Boyd, Harper W., Michael L. Ray and Edward C. Strong. "An
   Attitudinal Framework for Advertising Strategy," Journal of
   Marketing 36 (April 1972), 27-33.

7. Cohen, Joel B. "Toward an Integrated Use of Expectancy -
   Value Attitude Models," in G. David Hughes and Michael L.
   Ray, eds., Buyer/Consumer Information Processing. Chapel
   Hill: University of North Carolina Press, 1974.

8. Craik, F.M. and R.S. Lockhart. "Levels of Processing: A
   Framework for Memory Research," Journal of Verbal Learning

and Verbal Behavior 11 (December 1972), 156-163.

9. Engel, J.F., D.T. Kollat and R.D. Blackwell. Consumer Behavior. New York: Holt Reinhart and Winston, 1968.

10. Fishbein, Martin. "A Behavior Approach to the Relations Between Beliefs About an Object and the Attitude Toward the Object," in Martin Fishbein, ed., Readings in Attitude Theory and Measurement. New York: Wiley, 1967.

11. Harrell, Gilbert D. "Involvement in Product Class and Confidence in Beliefs about Brands as Potential Determinant of Attitudes - Behavioral Intent Relationships," in John C. Maloney and Bernard Silverman, eds., Attitude Research Plays for High Stakes. Chicago: American Marketing Association, 1978, forthcoming.

12. Howard, John A. and Jagdish N. Sheth. The Theory of Buyer Behavior. New York: John Wiley, 1969.

13. Hupfer, Nancy T. and David M. Gardner. "Differential Involvement with Products and Issues: An Exploratory Study," in David M. Gardner, ed., Proceedings, Association for Consumer Research. College Park: ACR, 1971, 262-269.

14. Kassarjian, Harold H. "Presidential Address," in H. Keith Hunt, ed., Advances in Consumer Research, Vol. 5. Ann Arbor: Association for Consumer Research, 1978.

15. Kassarjian, Harold H. and Waltraud M. Kassarjian. "Attitudes Under Low Involvement Conditions," in John C. Maloney and Bernard Silverman, eds., Attitude Research Plays for High Stakes. Chicago: American Marketing Association, 1978, forthcoming.

16. Katz, Daniel. "The Functional Approach to the Study of Attitudes," Public Opinion Quarterly 24 (1960), 163-204.

17. Krech, D., R.S. Crutchfield, and E. Ballachey. Individual in Society. New York: McGraw Hill, 1964.

18. Krugman, H.E. "The Impact of Television Advertising: Learning Without Involvement," Public Opinion Quarterly 29 (Fall 1965), 349-56.

19. Krugman, H.E. "The Learning of Consumer Likes, Preferences, an and Choices," in F. . Bass, C.W. King and E.A. Pessemier, eds., Applications of the Sciences in Marketing Management. New York: Wiley, 1968.

20. Krugman, Herbert E. "Low Involvement Theory in the Light of New Brain Research," in John C. Maloney and Bernard Silverman, eds., Attitude Research Plays for High Stakes. Chicago: American Marketing Association, 1978, forthcoming.

21. Lastovicka, John L. "A Manual for Scoring Unstructured Thoughts." Temple University Working Paper, 1978.

22. Lastovicka, John L. and Edward H. Bonfield. "Do Consumers Really Have Brand Attitudes?" Temple University Marketing Working Paper, 1978.

23. Lastovicka, John L. and David M. Gardner. "Low Involvement Versus High Involvement Cognitive Structures," in H. Keith Hunt, ed., Advances in Consumer Research, Vol. 5. Ann Arbor: Association for Consumer Research, 1978.

24. Lastovicka, John L. and David M. Gardner. "Components of Involvement," in John C. Maloney and Bernard Silverman, eds., Attitude Research Plays for High Stakes. Chicago: American Marketing Association, 1978, forthcoming.

25. Lutz, Richard J. "A Functional Approach to Consumer Attitude Research," in H. Keith Hunt, ed., Advances in Consumer Research, Vol. 5. Ann Arbor: Association for Consumer Research, 1978.

26. Martin, Rom J. "Motivation in Buyer Behavior Theory: From Mechanism to Cognition," in Arch G. Woodside et al., eds., Consumer and Industrial Buyer Behavior. New York: Elsevier, 1977.

27. Myers, James H. and William H. Reynolds. Consumer Behavior and Marketing Management. Boston: Houghton Mifflin, 1967.

28. Osgood, C.E., G.J. Suci, and P.H. Tannenbaum. The Measurement of Meaning. Urbana: University of Illinois Press, 1957.

29. Ray, M.L., A.G. Sawyer, M.L. Rothschild, R.M. Heeler, E.C. Strong and J.B. Reed. "Marketing Communications and the Hierarchy of Effects," in P. Clarke, ed., New Models for Mass Communication Research. Annual Review of Communication Research Series, Vol. 2. Beverly Hills: Sage Publications, Inc., 1973.

30. Ray, Michael L. and Peter H. Webb. "Three Learning Theory Traditions and Their Applications in Marketing," in R.C. Curhan, ed., 1974 Combined Proceedings. Chicago: American Marketing Association, 100-103.

31. Razran, Gregory. _Mind in Evolution: An East-West Synthesis of Learned Behavior and Cognition_. Boston: Houghton Mifflin, 1971.

32. Rhine, Ramon J. "A Concept-Formation Approach to Attitude Acquisition," _Psychological Review_, 65 (1958), 362-370.

33. Rosenberg, Milton J. "Cognitive Structure and Attitudinal Affect," _Journal of Abnormal and Social Psychology_, 53 (November 1956), 367-372.

34. Rothschild, Michael L. "Advertising Strategies for High and Low Involvement Situations," in John C. Maloney and Bernard Silverman, eds., _Attitude Research Plays for High Stakes_. Chicago: American Marketing Association, 1978, forthcoming.

35. Runyon, Kenneth E. _Consumer Behavior and the Practice of Marketing_. Columbus: Merrill, 1977, p. 282.

36. Ryan, Michael J. and Edward H. Bonfield. "The Fishbein Extended Model and Consumer Behavior," _Journal of Consumer Research_, 2 (September 1975), 118-132.

37. Scott, William A. "Attitude Measurement," in Gardner Lindsey and Elliot Aronson, eds., _The Handbook of Social Psychology_, Vol. 2: _Research Methods_. Reading: Addison-Wesley, 1968.

38. Skinner, B.F. _Beyond Freedom and Dignity_. New York: Knopf, 1972.

39. Smith, M. Brewster, J.S. Bruner and R.W. White. _Opinions and Personality_. New York: Wiley, 1956.

40. Sperry, R.W. "Lateral Specialization of Cerebral Function in the Surgically Separated Hemispheres," in Frank J. McGuigan and R.A. Schoonover, eds., _The Psychophysiology of Thinking, Studies of Covert Processes_. New York: Academic Press, 1973, 209-229.

41. Sudman, Seymour. "The Uses of Telephone Directories for Survey Sampling," _Journal of Marketing Research_, 10 (1973), 204-207.

42. Thurstone, Louis L. "The Measurement of Attitudes," _Journal of Abnormal and Social Psychology_, 26 (1931), 249-269.

43. Watson, John B. _Behaviorism_. New York: Norton, 1925.

ATTITUDINAL REACTIONS TO ADVERTISEMENTS

Mary Jane Schlinger
University of Illinois, Chicago Circle

INTRODUCTION

The Viewer Response Profile is a copytesting instrument designed to measure attitudinal responses to rough or finished television commercials, radio commercials, or print advertisements. The current Viewer Response Profile, which has been developed and used over the past eleven years by Leo Burnett Co., is composed of 52 word and sentence items. A respondent describes his or her reaction to an advertisement by rating each item on a six point disagree-to-agree scale.

The Viewer Response Profile instrument, its theory and its development research are described in a paper forthcoming in the Journal of Advertising Research [10]. The purpose here is to discuss some insights into copytesting and advertising that have been gleaned from experience with the VRP. As background to that discussion, six attitudinal dimensions measured by the Viewer Response Profile will be presented and briefly interpreted.

VIEWER RESPONSE PROFILE FACTORS

Repeated factor analyses of the Viewer Response Profile items have identified six stable factors. These factors, their "names" or labels, and items representing each are shown in Table 1. The loadings in Table 1 are derived from a factor analysis based on mean scores for 1626 storyboards and commercials. In most cases, each storyboard or commercial was rated by 30 respondents, although in a few instances the sample size was larger.

It should be noted that there have been and will continue to be variations in the words and sentences that comprise each factor dimension as old items occasionally are dropped and new items are incorporated into the instrument. Thus, there are minor differences between the factors reported in Table 1 and those shown in the forthcoming Journal of Advertising Research article.

The first two factors that will be discussed, Relevant News and Brand Reinforcement, have to do with reactions to the advertised brand. The remaining four -- Stimulation, Empathy, Familiarity, and Confusion -- measure responses to the commercial and its execution. The percentage of total variance accounted for by each factor is: Relevant News, 15%; Brand Reinforcement, 12%; Stimulation, 20%; Empathy, 14%; Familiarity, 6%; and Confusion, 6%.

Relevant News

Items that represent the Relevant News factor suggest that the advertisement and its messages were relevant to the viewers' needs. Besides statements of relevance, there are items which suggest: (1) learning of information ("The commercial gave me a new idea"); (2) information-seeking ("I would be interested in getting more information about the product"); curious disbeliever ("The commercial made me think I might try the brand -- just to see if it's as good as they say"); (3) cognitive dissonance ("The commercial reminded me that I'm dissatisfied with what I'm using now and I'm looking for something better"); (4) interest in trying ("The commercial told me about a product I think I'd like to try"); and (5) mental rehearsal of usage ("During the commercial I thought how that product might be useful for me").

TABLE 1

ITEMS REPRESENTING SIX VIEWER RESPONSE PROFILE FACTORS

Factor	Items	Loading on Factor (n=1626)
Relevant News	During the commercial I thought how that product might be useful for me.	.84
	The commercial gave me a new idea.	.81
	I would be interested in getting more information about the product.	.80
	The commercial showed me the product has certain advantages.	.76
	The commercial made me think I might try the brand--just to see if it's as good as they say.	.76
	Important for me.	.76

172

Factor	Items	Loading of Factor (n=1626)
Relevant News (cont'd.)	The commercial reminded me that I'm dissatisfied with what I'm using now and I'm looking for something better.	.73
	The commercial made me feel the product is right for me.	.73
	I learned something from the commercial that I didn't know before.	.70
	The commercial told me about a product I think I'd like to try.	.70
	The ad didn't have anything to do with me or my needs.	-.51
Brand Reinforcement	I know that the advertised brand is a dependable, reliable one.	.79
	That's a good brand, and I wouldn't hesitate recommending it to others.	.72
	The commercial described certain specific product characteristics that are undesirable to me.	-.55
	I found myself disagreeing with some things in the commercial.	-.67
	As I watched, I though of reasons why I would not buy the product.	-.69
	The commercial made exaggerated (and untrue) claims about the product.	-.72
	What they said about the product was dishonest.	-.78

Factor	Items	Loading of Factor (n=1626)
Stimulating	Amusing.	.87
	The commercial was lots of fun to watch and listen to.	.87
	Playful.	.86
	I thought it was clever and quite entertaining.	.86
	Exciting.	.83
	The characters (or persons) in the commercial capture your attention.	.82
	The enthusiasm of the commercial was catching.	.82
	Unique.	.75
	Tender.	.67
	Dreamy.	.61
	It was dull and boring.	-.66
Empathy	The commercial was very realistic -- that is, true to life.	.71
	I liked the commercial because it was personal and intimate.	.59
	I felt as thought I was right there in the commercial experiencing the same thing.	.55
	The commercial irritated me - it was annoying.	-.66
	In poor taste.	-.69
	I felt the commercial talked down to me.	-.74

Factor	Items	Loading of Factor (n=1626)
Empathy (cont'd.)	That ad insults my intelligence.	-.75
	It was an unrealistic ad - far-fetched.	-.77
	Silly.	-.89
Familiarity	Familiar.	.78
	I've seen this commercial so many times -- I'm tired of it.	.76
	Saw before.	.75
Confusion	It was too complex. I wasn't sure what was going on.	.80
	It required a lot of effort to follow the commercial.	.68
	I was so busy watching the screen, I didn't listen to the talk.	.57

Note: Items shown have loadings of ±.50 or greater on a single factor.

The Relevant News items indicate interest in the product and buying, but not necessarily conviction or persuasion. Presumably the viewer who rates a commercial high on Relevant News might try the brand and then formulate or change his attitude toward it, based on his experience. This is the type of reaction described by low involvement theory, which posits a think-do-feel or cognitive-conative-affective hierarchy of response [4, 8]. Such a response typology is congruent with the fact that most of the advertisements tested on the VRP are for food, beverage and drug products that probably are not involving for the majority of persons.

Although the Relevant News dimension may represent low involvement with the product, the nature of the items suggests some interest or involvement with the advertising. This interest probably is enhanced by the forced viewing situation and by the typical requirement that Viewer Response Profile respondents be users of the product category.

Brand Reinforcement

The second factor is labeled Brand Reinforcement because the positive statements imply that the advertising has reassured the viewer that the advertised brand is a good one. The Brand Reinforcement factor measures what is probably the most common reaction to advertising, the reinforcement of pre-existing attitudes. On the negative end, Brand Reinforcement statements point to out-right rejection of the brand and commercial. One sentence, "I found myself disagreeing with some things in the commercial," suggests counterarguing, and a couple of other items reflect disbelief.

The appearance of "disbelief" items on two uncorrelated factor dimensions, i.e., Relevant News and Brand Reinforcement, points to the complexity of "believability" as a concept, and emphasizes the difference between "curious disbelief" and "disbelief-rejection" [6]. Simplistic measures of advertising believability, such as ratings on the single item "believable," confound these two very different kinds of response.

Users of the advertised brand tend to score higher on Brand Reinforcement than nonusers. When a brand user has a high factor score it may indicate that the advertising reinforced his attitudes, whereas when a nonuser has a high factor score it could suggest attitude change (i.e., greater liking or preference).

Brand Reinforcement scores are affected not only by execution and usage but also by the nature of the product and the reputation of the advertised brand. Food advertisements, for example, are apt to generate higher scores than those for tobacco or drugs. And within a product category, brands with a more favorable image or larger brand share tend to be rated higher than those with a less favorable image.

Stimulation

"Enjoyable," "pleasant," "entertaining," and "active" are words that describe the response measured by the Stimulation factor. Items representing the positive pole of this dimension indicate that the advertisement was exciting, amusing, and different from other advertising. The opposite of a stimulating ad is one which is dull and boring.

A stimulating or entertaining execution is one way to "sugar coat" the persuasive message of an advertisement. Such a format also may attract attention and, in the case those few

176

campaigns that catch the popular imageination, generate publicity and word of mouth dissemination. Furthermore, the favorable affect associated with a likable commercial or print ad could be generalized to the brand.

But the brand name and message may get lost in a highly stimulating execution. When this happens, or when the execution is fragmented rather than coherently structured, Stimulation scores can correlate negatively with day after recall scores.

Empathy

The fourth factor is Empathy, and intuitively it seems to have three facets. The first is realism. The second is identification with an execution which mirrors some aspect of the viewer's self. And the third is rejection or dislike of the advertising execution.

It previously was noted that statements rejecting the advertised brand form the negative pole of the Brand Reinforcement factor. Thus it appears that rejection of the brand is independent from rejection of the advertising execution, since the two different judgments represent uncorrelated factor dimensions.

The negative statements on Empathy provide insight into why viewers dislike certain creative formats. Since disliking is the polar opposite of Empathy, the implication is that a viewer is irritated by executions that he finds incompatible with his experience and imagination. Such ads are described as unreal, insulting, boring and silly. Commercials described by negative Empathy go beyond the latitude of acceptance; viewers cannot engage in what Coleridge described as the "willing suspension of disbelief" which permits imaginative literature to be accepted even though it is not literally true.

Turning to the positive side of Empathy, commercials that score high often show realistic or idealized characters, situations, and interactions. Elements, such as the brand itself, music, scenery, etc., also can generate empathy. Furthermore, viewers can empathize with persons of the opposite sex, with fantasy, even with cartoon characters.

Familiarity and Confusion

In some cases, advertisements score high on the Familiarity factor because they have been exposed prior to copytesting and respondents have actually seen the ads before. However, there is a negative tone to this dimension, and an unexposed ad may generate relatively high Familiarity ratings if it utilizes a stereotyped format, if viewers are tired of the campaign that the ad represents, or if the ad is not noticeably different from others for the same brand.

Viewers describe advertisements above average on Confusion if they are busy, lack audio-visual congruence, or include distracting or poorly integrated elements.

Interpretation of Viewer Response Profile

Primarily the Viewer Response Profile is used as a diagnostic copytesting tool to identify potential strengths and weaknesses in rough or finished advertisements. There is no formula for interpreting VRP factor scores. In analyzing the data, the researcher must take into account the advertising strategy for the brand, creative goals, and the overall pattern of factor scores for the tested advertisement as well as scores for those ads with which it is being compared. Additional insights are gained by looking at ratings on the individual items that make up each factor.

The question sometimes is asked: "Is a high Stimulation, or Relevant News, or Brand Reinforcement, etc., score 'good'," and vice versa? There can be no simple answer to such a question because: (1) there are various reasons for advertising, and different kinds of advertisements attempt to elicit different kinds of response; (2) there is no one model of "effective" advertising that applies across all brands and situations; and, (3) it cannot be assumed that a high score on any one factor dimension is either a necessary or sufficient indicator of "effectiveness," however that term may be defined. For example, it is intuitively appealing to believe that a high Relevant News score is desirable, especially if the advertised brand is new, or the purpose of the advertising is to convey information. However, a high Relevant News score might not be sufficient, e.g., if the advertisement fails to attract attention. And much advertising seems to "work" without conveying substantive information.

The Viewer Response Profile can be used for evaluation where: (1) the copy strategy for a brand states that the advertising is intended to elicit a certain kind of response, e.g., humor, empathy, etc; (2) a statistical relationship between Viewer Response Profile item ratings for factor scores and criterion data for a brand has been established.

IMPLICATIONS FOR COPY TESTING

In the past three and a half years, more than 45,000 respondents used the VRP to describe their reactions to storyboards, commercials and print advertisements, thereby providing a rich data bank for learning both about copytesting and about advertising. The remainder of this paper will focus on selected findings gleaned from analyses of the VRP data. Like the traditional bride's costume, these findings or insights include some that are old, perhaps a few that are new and some that are borrowed (generally from recent theoretical insights into the way that advertising works).

One caution: most of the advertising tested on the Viewer Response Profile was produced by a single agency, Leo Burnett U.S.A. However, all large agencies represent a variety of clients and write in a diversity of creative styles. Although there may be (or may not be) distinct "schools" of advertising associated with one or another agency, there also is substantial cross-fertilization of creative ideas, both because innovative advertising campaigns have high visibility, and because of agency switches by creative personnel.

Turning to implications for copytesting that have been drawn from the Viewer Response Profile experience, it seems clear that one way to discover how people feel during and after seeing an advertisement is to ask them. The use of standardized rating scales, rather than open-ended questions or scales easily gathered and processed for advertisements within or across brand and product categories and executional styles. The emergence of six uncorrelated dimensions of response suggests that the Viewer Response Profile measures something more than simply liking or the halo effect generated by pleasant executions.

VRP Scales and Open-Ended Questions

At Leo Burnett, the VRP scales typically have been used in conjunction with open-ended questions that ask the respondent to describe the content of the advertising. Experience suggests that the scales and the questions yield complementary but different information. The verbatim descriptions of advertisement provided by open-ended questions allow analysis of the structure and coherence of each respondent's playback, examination of what specific elements of the message and content are recalled, and evaluation of such factors as to whether or not the brand name and message are integrated into the commercial narrative, whether certain executional elements are distracting, etc.

The VRP structured scales do not require respondents to articulate their feelings, and researchers do not have to subjectively code verbatim responses. The scales measure attitudes about the commercial and brand, or how respondents feel; the open-ended questions are geared toward communication or what viewers know. One measure is not a substitute for the other, though each helps confirm, check and explain the other.

Confusion

The Viewer Response Profile is not a sensitive way to measure confusion, since respondents may misinterpret advertisements without being aware that they are "confused". The Confusion factor only taps those instances when people are both aware that they are confused and willing to admit it. One suspects, therefore, that a high Confusion score may indicate communication chaos, and should serve as a warning to the advertiser that something may well be amiss, especially if the advertisement aims at a cognitive response or is scheduled for light media exposure.

Attitude Intensity

Several years ago, a measure of attitude intensity was appended to three Brand Reinforcement items in an effort to see if such a measure would make the items more discriminating. The intensity scale used is as follows:

How sure are you about the last rating?

1 - Extremely
2 - Very sure
3 - Fairly sure
4 - Not sure at all

Recently the results of the intensity measure were examined for two brands, a beverage and a household cleaner. Specifically, one way analyses of variance were performed on each of the three items across ten or more finished commercials for each brand, generating six F-ratios. These were compared with the beverage and cleaner commercials on the three Brand Reinforcement items, scored +3 to -3, multiplied times the 1-4 intensity ratings.

The results showed that Brand Reinforcement ratings alone got as high or higher F-ratios than Brand Reinforcement multiplied by intensity scores. These findings are preliminary in that other product categories could be examined, as could other ways of combining the scales. However, it appears that the intensity measure may not increase the sensitivity of the VRP items.

INSIGHTS INTO ADVERTISING

Experience with the VRP data reinforces the belief that there is no one model or formula for "effective" advertising. Advertising campaigns that are judged to be "good" often elicit differing response profiles, depending upon the product category, brand, competitive situation, stage in life-cycle, copy strategy, and so on. Also, when VRP scores are regressed against criterion scores, such as recall or pre-post attitude change, different relationships emerge not only for different criteria but also for different brands using the same criterion. Thus the VRP as well as other current research, such as that on hierarchies of effects models, suggest that the notion of a single model of advertising effectiveness is illusory [8].

Other topics which will be addressed in this section are: (1) reactions to print ads versus TV commercials; (2) advertising and public opinion; (3) the positive rewards that advertising provides for its audiences; and (4) overall patterns of response to TV commercials.

Print Ads Versus TV Commercials

In order to better understand how people respond to print versus TV advertising, overall mean scores for 151 magazine ads and 39 30-second commercials, each rated by 30 respondents, were subjected to item by item t-tests.

The print and TV executions represented in this study were not matched; nor were the same brands represented in each sample of advertisements, since some brands advertise exclusively in print, and vice versa.

Table 2 shows those VRP items for which the print mean scores were significantly higher than the TV means. These data indicate that print is described as the more confusing medium. In part, this difference may be an artifact of the copytesting situation; exposure to the print ads sometimes was restricted to ten seconds or so. However, there is common sense support for the validity of the difference in that: (1) Reading requires more effort than TV viewing, and the average American is not a highly skilled reader; and (2) print commonly is used for material that is considered too lengthy or technical for the electronic media. Another interpretation of the difference in confusion, of course, could be that there is a need for greater clarity and simplicity in print advertising.

Print ads are relatively dull and boring. Put differ-

TABLE 2

SIGNIFICANT DIFFERENCES: PRINT ADS VERSUS TV COMMERCIALS

Scales (Print version)	Print $\bar{X}$ (n=151)	TV $\bar{X}$ (n=391)	t-value
It was too complex.	2.42	1.94	18.10**
It was dull and boring.	3.00	2.50	11.91**
I was so busy looking at the picture that I didn't read the words.	3.12	2.76	8.65**
It required a lot of effort to understand the ad.	2.68	2.40	7.72**
I learned something from the ad that I didn't know before.	3.47	3.03	6.66**
The ad made me think of reasons why I would not buy this product.	2.73	2.45	6.55**
The ad made exaggerated (and untrue) claims about the product.	2.49	2.32	5.92**
What they said about the product is dishonest.	2.31	2.15	5.38**
In poor taste.	2.35	2.21	4.06**
I felt that the ad was describing how I feel at times.	3.33	3.17	3.02**
I found myself disagreeing with some things in the ad.	2.97	2.88	2.42*
The ad irritated me - it is annoying.	2.40	2.31	2.24*

*p < .05
**p < .01

ently, commercials, with their movement and sound, are more stimulating than magazine ads. In fact, though the data are not shown, the commercials produced significantly higher mean scores on every one of the positive items representing the Stimulation factor. On the other hand, respondents are more apt to feel that they have learned something from a print ad than a TV commercial.

Print ads seem to generate more counterarguing than TV commercials, i.e., respondents indicate that they are more inclined to disagree with things in the commercial and to think of reasons not to buy the product. This difference is congruent with Krugman's view that print is relatively high involvement, rational, "think-before-you-act" medium which taps left brain functions, whereas TV is low involvement, imagistic, and passive [4].

Finally, it was unexpected to find print ads scoring higher than television commercials on a number of negative items describing the ads as "exaggerated," "dishonest," "in poor taste" and "annoying". One possible explanation is that the interruptiveness and cluttered surroundings of TV commercials are as important or even more important in generating irritation and rejection than the commercial executions per se. Irritation attributable to the commercial environment would not be reflected in the VRP copytests since each respondent saw only one commercial. Also, if magazine ads contain more information than commercials, they may be more vulnerable to accusations of exaggeration and dishonesty.

It should be emphasized that the differences between the media on negative items are relative; the actual means of the items are below the mid-point of the scale (3.5) for both print and TV advertising, i.e., respondents tended to disagree with them.

Advertising and Public Opinion

Public opinion polls frequently have shown that Americans have negative attitudes toward advertising, especially TV commercials. For example, results of a 1964 study commissioned by the American Association of Advertising Agencies showed that: 48% of the sample had unfavorable or mixed attitudes toward advertising; 65% agreed that advertising often persuades people to buy things they should not buy; 43% said most advertising insults the intelligence of the average consumer; and 53% completely or partially rejected the idea that advertisements present a true picture of the product advertised [1].

In a 1967 Roper poll, 37% of the respondents indicated

either that they disliked practically all commercials or found most of them annoying, and 69% agreed that many commercials are done in poor taste [9]. A 1970 survey of attitudes toward television showed that 43% of the people interviewed generally agreed with the statement, "Commercials are generally in poor taste and very annoying" [2]. More recently, a 1976 opinion research study commissioned by Sentry Insurance showed that 46% of the public felt that all or most of TV advertising is seriously misleading, and 28% felt that same way about print ads [3].

VRP copytest results, on the other hand, indicate that most respondents reject statements describing the ads as annoying and dishonest. This was apparent from the data reported in the previous section on responses to TV versus print ads. Also, a tabluation of mean scores for 1255 commercials and storyboards shows that very few scored above the 3.5 mean of the 1 to 6 point scale on the following negative items:

Item	% of Commercials/Storyboards with $\bar{X}$ scores 3.5 or higher (n = 1255)
That ad insults my intelligence.	14
Silly.	11
What they said about the product was dishonest.	10
The commercial irritated me -- it was annoying.	2
In poor taste.	1
The commercial made exaggerated (and untrue) claims about the product.	0
I felt the commercial talked down to me.	0

This picture does not change when one examines ratings by individual VRP respondents. A tabulation of commercial and storyboard VRP ratings by 32,667 viewers yields the following distribution:

Percent of Respondents Who:

	Strongly Disagree/ Disagree	Somewhat Disagree	Somewhat Agree	Strongly Agree/ Agree
I felt the commercial talked down to me.	62	20	14	13
Silly.	53	15	16	16
That ad insults my intelligence.	54	19	14	13
The commercial irritated me - it was annoying.	64	12	13	11
In poor taste.	70	13	10	7
The commercial made exaggerated (and untrue) claims about the product.	68	20	8	4
What they said about the product was dishonest.	74	16	6	3

Clearly the majority of VRP respondents felt that the commercial or storyboard which they saw was honest, not exaggerated, tasteful and nonirritating. It also is clear that there is a great deal of difference between the poll results and the VRP copytest data. Americans appear to be much more critical of advertising in the aggregate and abstract sense than they are of particular commercials shown in a copytest.

This conclusion is supported by data from the previously mentioned Four A's study on consumer judgment of advertising. Although respondents expressed fairly high levels of general negative attitudes toward advertising, they classified only 4% of the advertisements that they actually paid attention to in the media as annoying or offensive [1].

In short, consumers seem to like commercials but dislike advertising.

Why the discrepancy? Perhaps advertising is a convenient "whipping boy." Perhaps people in opinion polls see agreement with statements critical of advertising as the socially desir-

185

able or expected response, and _vice versa_ in the copytest situation. Or perhaps the commercials that people judge offensive have more impact on their overall feelings about advertising than the unoffensive ones.

Positive Rewards of Advertising

In recent years, many articles have been published both in the popular and scholarly literature about the negative rewards and effects of advertising. The positive rewards that advertising offers its audiences are less frequently discussed, though nonetheless real. That the latter exists is best demonstrated by physiological measures which record how hard respondents will "work" (e.g., press buttons or levers, paddle, etc.) in order to see or hear an advertisement [5, 7, 11]. The fact that respondents do work indicates that the stimuli are reinforcing, and the fact that different ads elicit different levels of effort suggests that some are more rewarding than others.

The VRP factor structure defines various ways in which commercials reinforce viewing. These positive rewards include: humor; entertainment; excitement; self-enhancing empathy or identification; arousal of warm, tender feelings; opportunity for mental trial or usage of the brand; product news and information; incidental news or information, i.e., about fashions, home-decorating, etc.,; depiction or definition of real and ideal situations, interactions, environments; reiteration of relevant claims; reminder of the need to buy; stimulation of problem recognition; and reinforcement of brand choice but are not limited to the traditional product information function.

On the negative side, commercials "turn off" their viewers when they: are irrelevant to the person's needs; elicit disenhancing identification; bore, irritate, insult, or confuse; exhibit bad taste; or are overly-exposed.

Overall Patterns of Response

Viewer Response Profile ratings by 2100 respondents of 70 TV commercials and storyboards were subjected to inverse factor analysis in order to examine overall patterns of response. Previous split half analyses of the data had indicated that five orthogonal Q-factors were reliable, so that is the number obtained.

Table 3 shows item score deviations from the mean for each of the five groups, and the following descriptions are based on these data.

TABLE 3

Q-FACTOR DEVIATIONS FROM OVERALL MEANS

R-Factor Label	Items	Q-Factor Deviations					Overall Mean
		1 (n=1242)	2 (n=419)	3 (n=176)	4 (n=160)	5 (n=103)	(n=2100)
Relevant News	During the commercial I thought how that product might be useful for me.	.68	-.90	-1.48	-.99	-.55	4.03
	The commercial gave me a new idea.	.62	-.84	-1.15	-.62	-1.18	3.25
	I would be interested in getting more information about the product.	.62	-.61	-1.29	-1.27	-.77	3.61
	The commercial showed me the product has certain advantages.	.42	-.74	-.91	-.13	-.25	4.31
	The commercial made me think I might try the brand--just to see if it's as good as they say.	.75	-.97	-1.18	-1.41	-.91	3.86
	Important for me.	.63	-.90	-1.11	-1.06	-.37	3.57

TABLE 3 (cont'd.)

R-Factor Label	Items	Q-Factor Deviations					Overall Mean
		1 (n=1242)	2 (n=419)	3 (n=176)	4 (n=160)	5 (n=103)	(n=2100)
Relevant News (cont'd.)	The commercial reminded me that I'm dissatisfied with what I'm using now and I'm looking for something better.	.33	-.43	-.68	-.42	-.40	2.62
	The commercial made me feel the product is right for me.	.79	-1.02	-1.31	-1.60	-.72	3.55
	I learned something from the commercial that I didn't know before.	.45	-.71	-1.02	-.18	-1.05	3.20
	The commercial told me about a product I think I'd like to try.	.76	-.74	-1.57	-1.72	-.81	4.10
	The ad didn't have anything to do with me or my needs.	-.54	.74	1.00	1.15	.05	2.62

TABLE 3 (cont'd.)

R-Factor Label	Items	Q-Factor Deviations					Overall Mean
		1 (n=1242)	2 (n=419)	3 (n=176)	4 (n=160)	5 (n=103)	(n=2100)
Brand Reinforcement	I know that the advertised brand is a dependable, reliable one.	.27	-.30	-.31	-.91	-.12	4.76
	That's a good brand, and I wouldn't hesitate recommending it to others.	.54	-.57	-.89	-1.60	-.20	4.20
	The commercial described certain specific product characteristics that are undesirable to me.	-.25	.12	.48	1.03	.14	2.34
	I found myself disagreeing with some things in the commercial.	-.48	.74	.49	.98	.36	2.78
	As I watched, I thought of reasons why I would not buy the product.	-.47	.49	.66	1.67	.01	2.53
	The commercial exaggerated (and untrue) claims about the product.	-.28	.47	.31	.49	.14	2.23

189

TABLE 3 (cont'd.)

R-Factor Label	Items	Q-Factor Deviations					Overall Mean
		1 (n=1242)	2 (n=419)	3 (n=176)	4 (n=160)	5 (n=103)	(n=2100)
Brand Reinforcement (cont'd.)	What they said about the product was dishonest.	-.23	.33	.31	.44	.16	2.08
Stimulation	Amusing.	.57	-1.30	.65	-1.09	-.98	3.71
	The commercial was lots of fun to watch and listen to.	.72	-1.59	.29	-1.07	-.99	3.72
	Playful.	.45	-1.05	.73	-1.16	-.62	3.45
	I thought it was clever and quite entertaining.	.74	-1.70	.24	-.99	-.83	3.85
	Exciting.	.55	-1.14	.09	-.89	-.76	3.01
	The characters (or persons) in the commercial capture your attention.	.58	-1.47	.60	-.79	-.86	3.97
	The enthusiasm of the commercial is catching.	.69	-1.59	.21	-1.02	-.83	3.69

190

TABLE 3 (cont'd.)

R-Factor Label	Items	Q-Factor Deviations					Overall Mean
		1 (n=1242)	2 (n=419)	3 (n=176)	4 (n=160)	5 (n=103)	(n=2100)
Stimulation (cont'd.)	Unique.	.56	-1.13	.04	-.82	-.93	3.13
	Tender.	.55	-1.21	.00	-.77	-.49	2.99
	Dreamy.	.31	-.67	-.03	-.42	-.26	2.49
	It was dull and boring.	-.58	1.36	-.17	.67	.70	2.53
Empathy	The commercial was very realistic--that is, true to life.	.53	-1.23	-.84	-.04	.14	3.26
	I liked the commercial because it was personal and intimate.	.52	-1.13	-.27	-.65	-.16	2.99
	I felt as though I was right there in the commercial experiencing the same thing.	.63	-1.22	-.64	-.76	-.34	2.94
	The commercial irritated me--it was annoying.	-.56	-1.51	-.20	.41	.28	2.32

191

TABLE 3 (cont'd.)

R-Factor Label	Items	Q-Factor Deviations					Overall Mean
		1 (n=1242)	2 (n=419)	3 (n=176)	4 (n=160)	5 (n=103)	(n=2100)
Empathy (cont'd.)	In poor taste.	-.44	1.13	-.03	.42	.06	2.22
	I felt the commercial talked down to me.	-.40	1.08	.11	.00	.20	2.72
	That ad insults my intelligence.	-.54	1.30	.29	.23	.39	2.63
	It was an unrealistic ad--farfetched.	-.47	1.21	.55	.04	-.25	2.59
	Silly.	-.57	1.46	.46	.16	-.14	2.72
Famil-iarity	Familiar.	.07	-.56	.30	-.24	1.28	3.73
	I've seen this commercial so many times-- I'm tired of it.	-.29	.28	.28	.11	1.74	2.08
	Saw before.	-.08	-.42	.64	2.29	-.48	2.45
Confusion	It was too complex. I wasn't sure what was going on.	-.12	.29	.02	.20	.00	1.98

TABLE 3 (cont'd.)

R-Factor Label	Items	Q-Factor Deviations					Overall Mean
		1 (n=1242)	2 (n=419)	3 (n=176)	4 (n=160)	5 (n=103)	(n=2100)
Confusion (cont'd.)	It required a lot of effort to follow the commercial.	-.33	.93	.01	.18	-.03	2.47
	I was so busy watching the screen, I didn't listen to the talk.	-.03	.10	.18	-.04	-.25	2.77
Additional Items*	Soothing.	.51	-1.13	-.09	-.65	-.44	3.82
	I don't see how the product has much to do with what was being shown in the commercial.	-.36	.75	.53	.16	.08	2.27
	I will definitely buy the brand in the commercial.	.70	-.65	-1.36	-1.94	-.40	3.79
	What they showed didn't demonstrate the claims they were making about the product.	-.42	.89	.27	.48	.20	2.82

TABLE 3 (cont'd.)

| R-Factor Label | Items | Q-Factor Deviations | | | | | Overall Mean |
		1 (n=1242)	2 (n=419)	3 (n=176)	4 (n=160)	5 (n=103)	(n=2100)
Additional Items*	There's no real difference between the product shown and its competitors. They're all pretty much alike.	-.33	.43	.47	.65	.44	3.33
	The commercial strengthened my favorable views about the brand.	.66	-.96	-.89	-1.23	-.60	3.69
	I felt that the commercial was acting out what I feel like at times.	.57	-1.10	-.79	-.42	-.40	3.16
	This kind of commercial has been done so many times--it's the same old thing.	-.54	.91	.26	.77	1.16	3.14

* Do not represent any one factor

Factor 1, which accounts for 59% of the respondents, is highly favorable toward both the brand and the commercial. People representing this factor rate commercials above average on Relevant News, Stimulation, Brand Reinforcement and Empathy items. Of all the groups, this first one indicates the greatest interest in trying and buying the advertised product.

Factor 2 strongly rejects the commercial execution and is somewhat negative toward the brand. People in this group describe the commercial as irritating, confusing, dull, and unrealistic. They are less favorable toward the brand than two of the Q-factors (1, 5) but not as rejecting as the other two (3, 4). Factor 2, which includes 20% of the respondents, may represent the reaction generated by commercials which are heartily disliked but sometimes seem to "work", perhaps because they give the brand high visibility and the negative attitudes generated by the advertising are not generalized to the product.

Factor 3 type respondents enjoy the commercial but reject the brand. These respondents, who comprise 8% of the total, feel that although the commercials are amusing and playful, they also are irrelevant and unconvincing. This is the kind of response one would expect for commercials which entertain but fail to positively influence people's feelings about the brand.

Eight percent of the respondents formed Factor 4, which is characterized by negative attitudes toward the advertised brand. These people indicate that the commercial was irrelevant to their needs and they will not buy the advertised brand. They say that while viewing the commercial they argued with what was said and thought of reasons not to buy the product. Factor 4 has substantially lower mean scores on Brand Reinforcement items than the other factors. One cannot tell from the data to what extent their rejection of the brand pre-existed viewing or was generated by the commercials and story-boards.

The fifth factor - 5% of the viewers - describes the commercials as familiar, the "same old thing," uninformative and unstimulating. Yet they do not reject the brand; on the contrary, their scores on Brand Reinforcement items are about the same as those for the first factor. The advertisements described by this factor do not appear to be detracting from the brand's image, but they do not seem to be helping it much either.

The inverse factor analysis demonstrates two things. First, it quantifies certain modes of response that are more often the subject of speculation than demonstration, e.g., the humorous commercial that is unpersuasive and may distract attention from the brand. Second, the analysis indicates that responses to TV commercials are highly segmented. Examination of the factor loadings indicates that different people can have very different reactions to the same commercial. Not one of the 70 commercials and storyboards tested in the study eliminated a homogeneous reaction, i.e., where all 30 respondents who rated the stimulus had a .50 loading on one factor. All of the stimuli generated heterogeneous responses that generally were distributed across at least three and sometimes across all five dimensions. Thus it is meaningless to talk about the response to a commercial as if that were a matter of consensus; rather, there are varying levels of various patterns of reaction.

SUMMARY

This paper has described a copytesting instrument, the Viewer Response Profile, and reported selected findings derived from analysis fo VRP data, including the following: (1) in comparison with TV commercials, print advertisements are seen as relatively confusing, dull, and arguable, although respondents are more apt to agree that they learned something from a print ad than from a TV commercial; (2) people appear to express more negative attitudes toward advertising in public opinion polls, where they are asked about advertising in general, than they do in a copytesting situation where they are describing specific advertisements; and, (3) television commercials can provide a number of positive rewards for viewers such as humor and entertainment, the opportunity for self-enhancing empathy or identification, reinforcement of brand choice and usage, information about the brand, stimulation of problem recognition, etc.

REFERENCES

1. American Association of Advertising Agencies. The A.A.A.A. Study on Consumer Judgment of Advertising. New York: American Association of Advertising Agencies, May, 1965.

2. Bower, Robert T. Television and the Public. New York: Holt, Rinehart and Winston, 1973.

3. Consumerism at the Crossroads: A National Opinion Research Survey of Public, Activist, Business and Regulator Attitudes Toward the Consumer Movement. Sentry Insurance, 1976-77.

4. Krugman, H.E. "Low Involvement Theory in the Light of New Brain Research," in John C. Maloney (ed.), Attitude Research Plays for High Stakes. Chicago: American Marketing

Association, 1978. In press.

5. Lindsley, O.R. "A Behavioral Measure of Television View-
    ing," Journal of Advertising Research, 2 (September,
    1962), 2-12.

6. Maloney, John C. "Curiosity versus Disbelief in Adver-
    tising," Journal of Advertising Research, 2 (June, 1962),
    2-8.

7. Nathan, Peter E. and Wallace H. Wallace. "An Operant Be-
    havioral Measure of TV Commercial Effectiveness," Journal
    of Advertising Research, 5 (December, 1965), 13-20.

8. Ray, M.L., A.G. Sawyer, M.L. Rothschild, R.M. Heeler,
    E.C. Strong, and J.R. Reed. "Marketing Communication and
    the Hierarchy of Effects," in Peter Clarke (ed.), New
    Models for Mass Communication Research. Beverly Hills:
    Sage, 1973, 147-173.

9. Roper, Burns W. Emerging Profiles of Television and Other
    Mass Media: Public Attitudes 1959-1967, New York: Tele-
    vision Information Office, 1967.

10. Schlinger, Mary Jane. "A Viewer Response Profile for TV
    Commercials and Storyboards," Journal of Advertising Re-
    search. In press.

11. Wolf, Abraham, Dianne Z. Newman, and Lewis C. Winters.
    "Operant Measures of Interest as Related to Ad Lib Reader-
    ship," Journal of Advertising Research, 9 (June 1969),
    40-45.

PRINT: THE MESSAGE, THE MEDIUM, THE ENVIRONMENT

Carl Hixon and John Fiedler,
Leo Burnett U.S.A.

(Editor's Note: Carl Hixon and John Fiedler illustrated
their ideas with numerous slides of print ads. Unfortunately,
the printing process used for these proceedings does not lend
itself to clear reproduction of small photographs. In an attempt to convey some of the feeling of the original presentation, we have selected some of the ads with larger headlines
and distinct visual elements and included them with the text.)

Hixon: We'd like to begin by telling a historical anec-
dote: Ready? An Indian and a white man met. The white man
took a stick and drew a circle on the ground. "This," he said,
"is what the Indian knows." Then he drew a much larger circle
around it and said, "and this is what the white man knows."
The Indian took the stick and drew an enormous circle around
both. · "This is what no one knows," he said.

Fiedler: So much for what we know about print. The researcher knows what he can measure and sometimes deduce from
consumer behavior -- that's the smallest circle. The writer --
the master of medium -- knows more; he creates the message, he
knows what he feels. But there's more that none of us knows.

We've been trying to reassure ourselves about what we
thought we knew and at the same time explore some of the un-
knowns in that Indian's enormous circle. And that's what we'd
like to share with you.

Hixon: One trouble with the advertising business is that
-- at any particular moment -- we think we know so much. We've
got all knowledge neatly labeled and put away in little boxes.
Actually, what is truly known and quantifiable about persuasion
you could stick in your eye. For example, it's my impression
that the advertising business is far too smug in having pigeon-
holed the values and uses of print -- especially its creative
values and uses. So worrying that I might be as retarded as
the rest of the industry regarding print, perhaps because I've
been a Vice President too long, I went into the kitchen and
talked to the cooks. I queried the entire Leo Burnett Creative
Department in Chicago -- 350 writers and art directors, asking,
"When and why do you like using print?"

Some answers were matter-of-fact, some were innovative,
others were smart-alec and a few were downright mystical.

Fiedler: At the same time, with a somewhat smaller sample -- research budgets being what they are -- we talked to people who heavily and frequently read the various print media. We also reviewed much of the research literature on print. That small circle in the center.

We can't really talk about print in a vacuum. For most products -- cigarettes and liquor excepted -- it's only one component in a marketing and advertising mix. So we need to distinguish the differences between print and TV. Major differences which form the basis of our thinking about writing print, researching print. A consumer buys a television set, he cannot buy "print," that TV set is an electronic instrument that allows someone to access limited programming and its imbedded advertising in a predetermined sequence at predetermined times. Consumers, at least those without a VTR, have little control over the medium. That television set and much of the programming it brings into the home doesn't differentiate people, their needs, or how they relate to various products.

Hixon: Print's different. It's a number of media, not a single one. The audiences for these media are created by the editorial style and content of specific vehicles. Even within magazines, which are our focus this morning, there is far more diversity than watching television.

Fiedler: There's also tremendous growth. The number of magazine groups audited by ABC has increased from 252 in 1954 to 344 in 1977. Last year alone there were over 200 new magazine entries. Most of them are highly specialized, highly selective. Unlike television, people's access to print is specific and it's personal. With print your choice is early; you have to make a specific conscious decision to buy or subscribe. It's deliberate choice, the prices aren't cheap. It's personal because the range you have to choose from is marvelously large. Almost everyone accesses that range in a different way.

Different types of magazines are read for varying purposes. News magazines: people are reading the news magazines for information. That's what they want. They want to know what's going on in the world. People spoke to us in terms of it's being an encapsulated kind of a summary. "It tells me everything that's going on." A number of people said it's a super substitute for newspapers. "Once a week I go through, I get a summary of everything that's happening, I can read it quickly if I want to, but I know what's going on in the world. There's a summary of world events." But it was also interesting finding out why people do this.

Why does someone really need to know about world events

and what's happening? Among women, for example, there was a feeling of a need for social acceptance. "I don't want to appear a dummy in public," one said. A number of women read these magazines simply to have something for discussion in the evening. "I've got to know what's going on in the world so we can talk about it."

Other magazines satisfied other needs: escapism, home-making information, the need to be current in terms of being a female, information about hobbies and sports, and so on. The more specialized the magazines, the more reader involvement with what is going on. If I am a skiing enthusiast, I am going to buy a skiing magazine; I am really involved with that. It is a narrow special interest kind of an area, and it is a source of intense involvement to the people who read these magazines and the way they go through them. We found that the way people relate to advertising in special interest publications was very different to the way they relate to advertising in the more general magazine publication. There's often a blur between editorial content and advertising. Both are highly informative; both often read with the same level of interest.

This leads to a key differentiation between TV and print. The reading of a print vehicle is active and involving. With a magazine, with a newspaper, whatever it is, you actually. . . you really have to do something. One of the things you have to do is concentrate, and pay attention. You have to physically do something with your hands, whereas television is really very passive. Here's how people talked to us about the differences. With television "it does it all for you." "It's wonderful. I just go home, I lie on my bed, I turn the thing on and it's marvelous." "I don't have to do a thing." "The beautiful, wonderful world of escape." And this next comment was actually made by a person with a certain amount of glee and enthusiasm: "I can make a magazine work when I want it to. I control it. I'm not being controlled by these other things." So thinking about the active role of reading and the passive role of watching television, is, in fact, the major environmental difference between the media.

So the elements of selectivity, personal control, and choice criteria that are exerted in print media may result in less intrusive advertising in print than in television. People do not generally buy magazines to sit and read our ads. I am not saying that they have a negative attitude toward the advertising, but they are simply not buying the magazines to read the ads. They are easy to escape: one need only turn the page. Television commercials, by contrast, are not all that easy to escape. People talked to us about this: "You're relaxed and you don't feel like moving, so you sit and you watch the commercials." "You don't really have enough time to do something else. You can't get up and go away and come back again. It's going to take too long." "If you're interested in a program, you don't want to miss the continuation." So, many sit there and watch the advertising. There's almost a sense that people see the advertising as a pennance, the penalty of watching television. But with print, "I can skip the ads." It's as simple as that. No one needs to consciously expose himself to any print advertising whatever.

It's not an easy task to avoid all that advertising, though. In the last three years magazine ads pages have increased 18%; food ad pages are up 42% in the same period. Roughly half of all magazine pages are now advertising.

Enough for now about the environment and all those readers I talked to. What did some of your writers say about print?

Hixon: Here's one I liked: "<u>Nothing brands like print</u>."

Nothing brands like print. To begin with, I find that one of the commonest faults in creative work today is <u>underbranding</u>. No matter how <u>impactful</u> your advertising, if you fail to <u>brand</u> properly, you <u>lose</u>. Branding in <u>TV</u> can be tricky, and often we think we have when we haven't. TV branding must happen in a time sequence, frame by frame, second by second, and what may look like a big bold signature or package setting at the end of a storyboard actually represents only a moment of fleeting impression, plus some in-use glimpses upstream and a few voice-over mentions. Just a slam of the backdoor. Slam! What was that? I dunno!

But <u>print</u> branding!

Unmistakeable!

Hard to confuse with anything else.

In print, the branding becomes part of the whole visual experience, something permanent. It holds still while the ad goes on all around it and if the art director has done his duty the reader never loses sight of it. How lovely.

Fiedler: Not only is branding important; it's not always done as well as the last few ads show. Recognition and recall measures both provide insights into how an ad is branded. Starch Noting Scores average around 50%; Gallup & Robinson Proven Name Recall Scores average 10%. Some recent experimental research addressed the branding issue another way. Could users of a product category correctly identify the advertiser when the brand name -- that and nothing else -- was removed from the copy and package shot. There was a lot variability, but most brands did not create a look and feel all that unique. Fewer than a sixth of the ads were correctly identified by more than three-quarters of the readers.

Hixon: When else did the creative guys, or girls -- persons -- say they like using print?

"When the product has a print soul."

And when might that be? Well, when the subject is print itself.

Or when it has a still-life character.

Or when the product's inherent drama expressed itself most naturally in some established print idion -- a cartoon strip, for example.

Fiedler: My turn to show some ads; apologies, Carl! A little confusing. Difficult to count the number of elements here.

A lot simpler, and to me, a lot more appetizing.

"Print Soul"...I'm not sure I know how to measure it. In a depth interview, one respondent characterized his magazine reading. "It's elevating, I am accomplishing something." Another said, "There are no stupid voices in a magazine."

Hixon: All right what else did creatives say?

"When my copy runneth over."

Sometimes no amount of compression will fit the sale into

thirty seconds of TV exposure without turning it into a totally different animal. You hear it said about long copy that
"more is less" and that Winston Churchill asked for all staff
reports to be complete on just one page. Now if he had really
believed this he would have said, "We owe a lot to the RAF."
No, more is usually (often) more.

Fiedler: There's a paradox here. I was intrigued by a
woman's comment about why she read those ads which caught her
fancy. "They go into much more detail, you can really get involved." At the same time simplicity is key. Two-thirds noted
ads with fewer than five elements; only half as many (32%) when
there were ten or more elements.

Hixon: What else.

"When the television legals are after me."

A pragmatic reason, but good. The rules governing what
must be said or shown, at times make it impossible to state
yourself succinctly on television, if at all.

Another Burnett creative guy says:

"When I want complete control over production of the
finished advertisement."

This sounds like an art director talking, and he's com-
plaining about the difficulty of a creative man being able to
follow through in detail on his creation when it takes the form
of film. In most agencies his script and storyboard are fed
into a conveyor system and along a distant assembly line of
various TV artisans -- producers, directors, editors and such --
each of whom may see it quite differently from its creator, so
that the finished article resembles a kind of tin woodsman.

In contrast to this, a print ad can be mothered every step
of the way by an art director and his personal suppliers, and
is seldom in danger of corruption or "improvement" by people
who may not share his vision.

Another Burnetter observed:

"You can't pin a commercial on your wall."

I think he thought he was being arch in referring to the
typical creative man's pride of authorship, which of course
should have nothing to do with choice of medium. But the profound truth is that print does have permanence - a life after
death, sort of. TV is a magic shadow that flickers and is gone

without a trace but a print ad lasts as long as the paper and the ink, and this lends psychic substance to an idea, which I think is of value.

Fiedler: We didn't find too many people talking about pinning ads to the wall. Print does offer the reader some comparable rewards. "To cut out the centerfold," was one man's answer to my question as to why he read his favorite magazine. I never did find out if he read it or pinned it on his wall.

Hixon: Another creative person says:

"It's a terrible burden to have to persuade someone in 30 seconds."

Imagine a mugger putting a gun to your head and saying, You money or your life -- choose -- you've got 30 seconds." You don't have any money so now you've got 30 seconds to plead your case. I'd a damn sight rather have a well-written 2 page spread on the subject all ready to go in my back pocket and say, "Here, sir - read this."

I think we often confuse communication with persuasion. We take 30 seconds to repeatedly burn in some proposition like "Guinness is good for you" or whatever, and when the research shows that people can play it back we think we've won. Come on. Conviction is a feeling and not a fact. It seeps in slowly through various organs -- the heart, the stomach, the spleen -- and gradually softens your resistance. It seldom overwhelms you in a 30 second rush, like a Billy Graham conversion.

Fiedler: I never thought any of us could argue someone into buying a product. In fact much of what John Lastovicka said (see his paper in these Proceedings) reinforces the value of "Friendly Persuasion" as opposed to a more hard sell. Fortunately, the job of much advertising is not to persuade, but rather to reward the viewer...for reading the copy...for buying my brand. Sometimes we stand in our own way. We end up with very complex ads that at best confuse the reader. I don't think a confusing headline will tease the reader into the copy. In fact, the greater the effort required to see what the ad is about, the more difficult it is for the ad to seem to offer a reward commensurate with that effort.

Hixon: Yet another creative man says:

"I like print when a very simple idea can be posterized."

Some basic arithmetic posterized.

A poster about a user image.

The user image which started it all in the cigarette business.

When an idea is telegraphic, assumptive, and needs very little qualification it's bound to be a natural born print idea. And one which will bear a lot repetition, not to mention imitation.

Fiedler: We may under estimate the visual communications import of print. Gallup & Robinson found that ads where the illustration told little or nothing of the story were recalled 27% below norm; those which worked hard to tell the ad's story scored 32% above the norm. Print has the advantage of powerful photography; it seems to work. Ads with photography were 48% more likely to be recalled than those with line drawing. This advantage -- close up, real, color -- has tremendous impact.

For example, here are some simple, totally integrated, visually dominant ads.

Hixon: Here's another creative quote.

"I like using print when you can't even recite the strategy in 30 seconds."

The obvious answer is to point out that strategies which
cannot be executed in the chosen medium are non-strategies. So
go ye back and ponder it once more. Nevertheless it sometimes
happens that clients or their agencies in an excess of strategic zeal or perhaps naiveté will create a strategic monster
which is unworkable in television terms and then print is the
only alternative left to the wretched executor. Fortunately
this is a self-purifying stream as such strategies seldom suc-
ceed in any medium.

Yet another.

"When I want to touch the conscience of my audience."

A very perceptive statement with which I agree. I think a
lot of this conscience appeal has to do with the intimacy of
print, and the rest with the moral overtones of the medium viz
a viz television. Sitting alone with a magazine in your hands
-- actually touching it -- you are capable of an introspection
and a contemplation of the moment which is not possible in the
act of television viewing. Your conscience is more apt to be
nearer the surface at that moment, perhaps with its periscope
up.

Also, even with its sometimes prurient content, print
still has a character of public service and of information, and

209

has a powerful link with law, and academia, and liturgy -- unlike TV which derives almost entirely from show business. So,
print does have a special way of touching the conscience, and
this has commercial as well as charitable uses.

Fiedler: One reader characterized it this way: "Magazines are so different in content, and I am looking for different things."

Hixon: Among the smart-alec replies to my question, one
was a standout. I asked, "When do you prefer using print?" and
someone answered:

"When I'm selling hearing aids."

Another guy had said "When I want to use a nude" but that
was a bit obvious, and pretty tame stuff these days.

What other insights came out of the Creative Department?
This:

"I use print when I need a 'touch of class,' because television seems to make all things common."

How true when it's pointed out. There is a sophistication
to print -- even the crummiest print -- which TV can't match.
To begin with, print assumes that you can read, rather than
simply see and hear. Beyond that it assumes that you have
identified with some interest group and are responsive to information, rather than just stroking. Which means that in the
appropriate magazines you can address your audience with ads
like these:

You can communicate snooty things like this about your product and know that you are appearing in an ambiance which is complimentary to your tone of voice. You can choose your company in print but <u>not</u> in television. Networks have non-committal personalities.

Well, these were just some of the observations on print triggered by my question. Obviously to see into the soul of print it helps to know about print writing and print writers... print art directors, too.

In a perfect world every copywriter should be a generalist, at home in every medium; but in the real world most writers today have big TV chromosomes and tiny print chromosomes because our culture turns them out this way. Saul Bellow, who recently won the Nobel Prize for literature, is in his 60's while most of today's best known film writers and directors are in their 20's and 30's.

Any good advertising agency, however, should contain enough ink-stained wretches of the type I grew up with to write you a classy print campaign. Their presence in the Creative Department tells you it is a first rate shop.

A print-chromosomed copywriter has a second sight into his medium. He knows that out there between all those pages are creative opportunities of cosmic proportions, but he worries that everyone is too narrow-minded or chicken-hearted to try them. He understands the atmospherics of sending and receiving print messages, and in an age which fancies itself filmic, this knowledge troubles him. James Thurber of the <u>New Yorker</u> once noted that men who write for magazines walk with their heads down and their hands in their pockets, and that newspapers blow out of alleys and wrap around their legs. My guess is that this nervousness comes from worrying that one might be an endangered species.

So, what are some of these special insights he has into the print medium?

Well, to begin with, he understands that what a magazine does best is surround us with beloved objects, and with information on how to use them. The hunter is presented with his guns and dogs, the smoker with his pipes, the motorist with tires and tachometers, the single girl with her special life style accountrements and so forth, all pieced out with information on how to use and appreciate these yummy things, so that reading a magazine we become like gleeful little kids. This is the mood in which the print copywriter can court us -- when we're full of loverly, selfish feelings and wanting intimate things to be divulged.

The print writer understands that, in print, <u>gentleness</u> can be a virtue and <u>subtlety</u> can be a persuasive tool. Ideas that we privately approve but hesitate to recommend for television because they lack "bite" or "grab" often flower profitably in some quiet meadow of print, where they can solicit the reader with sweet reasonableness and sanity.

The print copywriter also knows that many products simply don't come to life in 30 seconds. It's not that they are complicated and need explaining but that they exist on a grander scale and must be contemplated for longer. Anything less fails to express their inherent drama. When the average TV commercial wilted to 30 seconds I suspect some natural law kicked in to make print that much more potent by way of redressing the balance. Besides being "expansive" in print you can be baroque. You can grapple the reader to the ad with dozens of Lilliputian attractions, making the sale bit by bit, with or without a dominant proposition. Like this:

The ability to swarm all over a reader is an exclusive property of print. In the hands of a gifted copywriter and art director it is worth a dozen finely focused commercials.

What's more, the print writer working at his leisurely craft has at his disposal every classic apparatus of the storyteller, from Homer to Kurt Vonnegut, Jr., while the film writer -- poor guy -- aches to use Stanley Kubric's newest film business but finds most of it awkward in his tiny TV world.

The print writer knows his reader is a devoted fellow.

212

For proof, try interrupting someone deep into a magazine article. Television, on the contrary, is a shared and self-in-
terrupting experience. It competes for share of mind with
whatever else goes on in the room. It toys with the viewer's
good will, now offering him program material, now snatching it
away at some desperate moment, substituting a commercial. A
magazine gets round this by serving up the advertising as a
side dish, giving the reader his choice. Incidentally, Lord`
Thompson, who for years owned and operated the London Times,
once defined editorial matter: "What is editorial matter?"
he said. "It's the stuff between the ads."

The reader of print is likely to be more tolerant and for-
giving a person as well. He doesn't "boo" your bad ads, he
simply edits them out with his eye without hating you for 30
seconds.

The reader not only reads words, he actually likes words.
He probably collects books full of them. Who collects TV sets?

There are many other times when the creative pro prefers
to wear his print hat:

There is an authority, an officialness, to the printed
page.

A gut-felt urgency which no other medium can express.

Let's see, what else can you do exclusively with print? Well, in print, perhaps even more so than in television, if you don't know what you're doing you can thoroughly confuse and demoralize the reader.

I studied this ad for 5 minutes and didn't get it. I still don't get it. It reminds me of what a critic once said about a contemporary poet: "Although he has tortured the English language for years he has never succeeded in forcing it to reveal its meaning." Perhaps someone here today can explain this ad to me. John?

214

Fiedler: No. But it does reinforce something that comes up whenever we research a broad set of print ads. And that's the importance of efficiency of communication. Avoiding mental work for the reader. Communicate quickly to those who may not read the copy. Interest those who will read that copy to dig and get involved. Print seems to elicit that kind of involvement that will let ad work not only for three seconds, but thirty, maybe even three hundred. "You can put it down, come back to it, and it's still there," one woman told us. Another said, "When I'm reading, there's involvement. That's why my husband won't let me read when he is home."

Hixon: As an old print writer before I became an old television writer I can tell you that writing print is psychologically tougher than writing TV. You can't fake it. There she sits on the wall, matey -- warts and all. An artful presentation won't postpone the ash can, nor is there a collective responsibility shelter for the many collaborators on the finished product if disaster should strike. Don't look for cosmetic help from the director or music man, or even a free lunch. Don't expect any lucky accidents on the set. You're on your own. You and your ad -- both of you naked and vulnerable -- stand side by side in the glaring light of the conference room, awaiting summary judgment. Print writing builds men -- women, too -- I hasten to add.

Most beginning writers today have a blinkered bias towards television because they think their career tracks will be swifter and smoother in this medium. Not so, not so! This is unwise, actually, in a rapidly changing industry and society where some of the biggest advertising budgets are not spent principally, even exclusively, in non-broadcast media. A creative novice today should aim to be an all-court player or he'll never make it at most major agencies. At Burnett, for example, many of our greatest case histories have been and still are print intensive. No writer or art director can bill himself a pro if he has to holler for help when the media strategy comes up magazine or newspaper. I would never hire a creative man who was not an enthusiastic and literate wordsmith.

Finally, I read in the periodicals that the newest business school theory to explain the role of advertiisng in the western economy champions our profession (surprise!) because it distributes information to consumers which they would not otherwise get, and thereby decreases alleged monopoly power. So, as the original and still senior information dispenser, print looks stronger and stronger as a strategic medium. I think we'd better think it through again.

Thank you very much.